THE
LINE OF
CONTROL

ADVANCE PRAISE FOR THE BOOK

'Happymon Jacob's *The Line of Control* engagingly decodes the complexity of the Indo-Pak relationship, drawing on a refreshingly personalized account of his visit to the Pakistani side of the Line of Control, complemented by the nuanced analysis that has been a hallmark of this seasoned commentator. An insightful and objective assessment that consciously steers clear of histrionics, this book is a welcome addition to the literature on the subject'—Dr Shashi Tharoor, member of Parliament, Lok Sabha, from Thiruvananthapuram and chairman of the Parliamentary Standing Committee on External Affairs

'I started *The Line of Control* expecting a dry academic book but what I got was anything but that. Happymon brings alive the conflict and tensions between India and Pakistan by focusing on the human stories—the soldiers, the officers, the politicians, the people of the two countries are all part of the landscape. The Line of Control is about so much more than the wires, mines and gadgets that divide, it's about the people and how the reality of this line affects lives every single day. This book surprised me and moved me in equal measure. I for one am glad that Happymon went through the trouble of writing it'—Omar Abdullah, former chief minister, Jammu and Kashmir

'This book reminds me of my time on the Line of Control. As the brigade major of 4 AK brigade, I dealt with the ceasefire violations in the southern sector for three years—and that too soon after the '71 War. I am therefore familiar with all these grounds: cattle grazers, calls of duty and breaking of monotonies. Most importantly, however, we had to ensure that the trauma of the lost war did not suppress the spirit of our troops. Of course, some violations had to be initiated by us precisely to address that issue. In the meantime, it has gotten worse after the uprising of the early 1990s. What is significant in this study is that Professor Jacob humanizes this spectacle. Yes, political or psychological factors guide the policy, the perpetrators may exchange bonhomie during the flag meetings, to then move on to more peaceful places—but there is no end to the sufferings of the people. No wonder that the faith healers are their ultimate hope'—Asad Durrani, former director general of Military Intelligence and chief of the Inter-Services Intelligence, Pakistan Army

'When you have a worthy academic with such a wealth of experience in dealing with Jammu and Kashmir through interaction with both sides to the conflict, he can make that experience extremely useful by making serious attempts at understanding the nuts and bolts on ground. That intent took Happymon Jacob to the turbulent environment of the Line of Control (LoC), not only on the Indian side but also to the Pakistani side across the LoC. This outstanding book is a product of this rare endeavour to blend the academic and intellectual understanding of the complex LoC-related issues such as infiltration and cross-border firing, with practical aspects of soldiering at one of the most dangerous places on earth. A must-read for every scholar warrior in India, for deeper understanding of Pakistan and its ways in Jammu and Kashmir'—Lieutenant General (retd) Syed Ata Hasnain, former general officer commanding 15 Corps and military secretary, Indian Army

THE LINE OF CONTROL

TRAVELLING WITH THE INDIAN AND PAKISTANI ARMIES

HAPPYMON JACOB

PENGUIN
VIKING
An imprint of Penguin Random House

VIKING

USA | Canada | UK | Ireland | Australia
New Zealand | India | South Africa | China

Viking is part of the Penguin Random House group of companies
whose addresses can be found at global.penguinrandomhouse.com

Published by Penguin Random House India Pvt. Ltd
7th Floor, Infinity Tower C, DLF Cyber City,
Gurgaon 122 002, Haryana, India

First published in Viking by Penguin Random House India 2018

10 9 8 7 6 5 4 3 2 1

ISBN 9780670091270

Typeset in Sabon by Manipal Digital Systems, Manipal
Printed at Replika Press Pvt. Ltd, India

www.penguin.co.in

To Siddhartha, for asking me what a 'B-O-R-D-E-R' is and looking so bewildered when I tried explaining it to you.

Don't lose that bewilderment!

Contents

Prologue

December 2017

December 2017 wasn't remarkable for any particular reason, except perhaps to me. India and Pakistan played host to the usual milieu of relentless cross-border firing and selectively leaked secret meetings between their national security advisers (NSAs)—not unique by any standard. This was the age of violence, both within and between the two South Asian rivals. It wasn't anything special or distinctly worrisome: the two countries had gotten used to it by then. Most people referred to it with routine indifference, if they referred to it at all. Others vowed revenge, but from within the confines of television studios, of course. Young men in uniform died guarding the citizens of India, and Pakistan—those with inflated national egos and those without.

In reality, 2017 was the bloodiest year since the India–Pakistan ceasefire agreement came into effect in November 2003. Several dozens of Indian and Pakistani soldiers and civilians were killed and even more injured on the Line of Control (LoC). Ceasefire violations (CFVs) spiked alarmingly. Since 2014 (till the end of 2017), when the Hindu nationalist leader Narendra Modi led the Bharatiya Janata Party (BJP) to power in New Delhi, India reported 2408 ceasefire violations; and Pakistan reported 2915 violations. According to news reports, the Indian Army killed 138 Pakistani soldiers in 2017, and lost around twenty-eight of its own.[1] Young men continued to be mobilized by the two sides to be sent to the LoC, to kill and get killed.

The media got their drama as the two NSAs of Pakistan and India, Nasser Khan Janjua and Ajit Kumar Doval, men who had the ear of their respective prime ministers, scheduled a secret meeting at an undisclosed location in Bangkok on 26 December 2017. The retired general and the former spymaster had made it a habit to adjourn to Bangkok when things went south between their countries. The media houses loved the spectacle and the suspense. The meeting was covered for its theatre, not for its outcomes, of which there were none. Most of the 24X7 television channels had forgotten to ask hard questions. Why would they when nationalistic drama demonstrably raises Television Rating Points (TRPs)? To be fair, the nightly guardians of our national interest did ask probing questions of the hapless Opposition, most of whom ran for cover when the combined force of the mainstream media and the right-wing government took them to task.

The shelling, firing and killing continued apace. In the first three months of 2018 alone, Pakistan reported 900 violations and India 633. That is, India fired 267 times more than Pakistan.

What's the big deal about 633 violations? you might wonder. Each violation could comprise hundreds of thousands of shots from weapons ranging from AK-47s to heavy pieces of military artillery such as 130-mm mortar guns in an area of 20–50 square kilometres over a twenty-four-hour period. Statistics won't and, as a matter of fact, can't ascertain how many shots were actually fired. No one knows those numbers for sure. Not that it mattered. You don't count the raindrops when it pours.

The violence on the border had become routine. Some celebrated it; some ignored it as 'minor incidents'; and some used it to make electoral gains. The families of those killed on the line often refused to condemn the violence by their own side; and if at all they did, no one reported it. Even faint suggestions of standing down in times of national catharsis could lose you the much-needed eyeballs, and commercial advertisements. What then stood out was a disturbing consensus on retaliation, on sorting out the adversary. This was a classic case of manufacturing consent.[2]

Since the Ceasefire Agreement (CFA) of 2003, several hundreds of people have been killed and injured, with civilian habitats being pounded day in and day out. Since 2013, the final year of the Congress-led government, until early 2018, close to 140 Indian and Pakistani civilians have been caught in the crossfire and killed.[3] Each time firing broke out, vernacular TV screens[4] across the country would play video clips—with high-pitched background music that makes your heart beat faster—of heavy artillery raining down on the opponent's bunkers jubilantly; such images would almost completely eclipse the heart-rending scenes of the families of soldiers and civilians wailing over their dear departed. Jubilation over killing Pakistanis trumped the tragedy of Indian deaths. Needless to mention that no clips of the 'enemy' pounding the Indian Army's forward posts made it to the newsrooms.

History tells us that violence, when normalized, can make societies behave monstrously, and civilizational progress, it could be said, is directly proportional to the extent of legitimacy that exists in a society for violence.

Personally, for me, however, early December 2017 was eventful. Under this umbrella of smoke and cross-LoC violence, the Pakistan Army had agreed to take me on a tour of the LoC—the de facto border whose acronym, what with the almost quotidian artillery exchange, could easily stand for Line of Crossfire.

I had been to Pakistan several times, including Pakistan-Occupied Kashmir (PoK), but not to the LoC. A journey with the Pakistan Army officers within the firing range of the Indian Army—this was to be the most adventurous journey of my life.

Close to one and a half years before the authorities at Rawalpindi gave me the green signal for a visit, I also spent about a month on the Indian side of the India–Pakistan border. I was accompanying the Indian Army and the Border Security Force (BSF), a paramilitary organization that mans the International Border (IB) with Pakistan.

Besides being an intellectual pilgrimage, travelling with the men in uniform along the site of one of the most treacherous theatres of conflict in the world also turned out to be a lesson in humanism, one that touched me deeply and personally. To be able to view the LoC from both sides is what made it riveting. And experiencing the two sides of a live, bloody conflict transforms one's understanding of conflicts, in an irrecoverable way, even for an academic whose job it was to study conflicts.

I had to make that trip to be able to write and speak convincingly about the LoC. I had a great deal of trepidation about what awaited me on the Pakistan side.

This book is the story of that gripping journey.

1

Inside the Enemy Territory

'We Know All about You'

'I thought this was a meat-eating country.'

'Well, since you don't eat meat,' said the friendly colonel, 'we're all eating fish today.' The dinner spread at the Muzaffarabad army officers' mess, at the top of a steep hill, intrigued me.

'How do you know I'm pescatarian?' I had given up meat not too long ago.

'We know all about you,' he said.

The Pakistani colonel wasn't kidding, despite the knowing smile on his face. The men around him stood motionless, waiting for him to sit down, and would not smile at his revelation. He asked me to sit at the head of the table. 'This is your den, Tiger,' I replied, referring to his moniker which I'd heard just a few moments ago.

The colonel meant what he said. All the Pakistani army officers present in the officers' mess at the Muzaffarabad brigade headquarters (HQ) had fish that day. Through the 8 p.m. dinner, I was the one doing most of the talking. The colonel listened patiently, and the other officers stared down at their food. In retrospect, I think much of that could be explained by anxiety. People talk when they are tense. His seemingly half-serious suggestion had startled me to the core.

For someone who grew up in the southern Indian state of Kerala and lived there for over fifteen years, the fish curry—especially some nondescript river fish in over-spiced, runny gravy—was boring. But the gesture definitely wasn't. Does it matter even if the gesture was excessively superfluous? Not eating meat on my behalf did seem a little over the top though.

But that's not the point.

Boring fish curry wasn't enough to kill my curiosity: How on earth did they know I was a pescatarian? What did the colonel even mean by 'We know all about you'? Did they? Really? Not that I was an extremely secretive person. Sure, I was a social media enthusiast, but I didn't post my food preferences online. Perhaps he was playing a prank on me. Hadn't there been a smile on his face when he said this?

This theory brought me a fleeting sense of relief, which of course vanished pretty quickly. The colonel's comment had left me feeling edgy—coming as it did at the fag end of a cold December evening, at a Pakistani military base in PoK, not too far from where they were targeting the Indian Army posts with medium and field artillery.

My Indian SIM card had stopped working, obviously. No Internet. The Pakistan Army was yet to loan me a local SIM card. My home was just about 700 kilometres away. Uri, the closest Indian city in Kashmir, was only 60 kilometres—and yet, I felt a long way from home. Outside, the two forces were constantly raining bullets and shells on each other.

Almost nothing seemed to be in my control. I was surrounded by 'enemy' forces, deep inside the enemy territory. To make matters worse, that 'We know all about you' kept ringing in my ear, well into the night, in my room at the mess. I slept in the guest house perched at the top of the mountain just below the brigadier's house—an indication, perhaps, of the fact that the Pakistan Army had decided to take good care of the guest from the enemy country.

It was a long, cold and tense night. The snowy mountain peaks glistened in the moonlight as the wind argued with the trees all through the night. But I was too preoccupied for such worldly pleasures.

In the days that followed, I would ask the colonel how much and what he knew about me. Though I tried to keep my queries light-hearted, they were almost always tinged with seriousness. Maybe they had a file on me at their famed Inter-Services Intelligence (ISI) HQ in Aabpara in suburban Islamabad. He would laugh at my suggestion without saying a thing, as if I were a child asking silly questions.

I had spent over two years trying to get invited to the Pakistani side of the LoC. Here I was at the army mess in PoK getting to mingle with the soldiers and hear their take on the situation. Personally, and professionally, this meant a lot to me, since I had already spent time with the Indian Army on the other side of the LoC.

'*Bhaiyya*, shall I get you some green tea?' The non-combatant bearer of the Pakistan Army (they had abandoned the batman system since the time of General Musharraf) wasn't sure how to address the talkative man from the other side. He was used to addressing army officers. 'With some honey in it?' he asked after a pause.

The snow-capped mountains, forming lush green valleys through which serpentine roads made their way, felt like nature's cover-up for what was really going on. A fragile sense of normality. Behind the beauty of those high ranges, the sound of gunshots replaced the chirping of crickets, night after night, not too far from the LoC.

There was deception in the air.

The Lost Ardbeg

The peaty, smoky Ardbeg is a fine Scottish single malt and has been one of my favourites ever since I could afford a single malt once in a while—though I wasn't exactly eulogizing its virtues to the overworked, uninterested customs officer at Lahore's Allama Iqbal International Airport when he asked me to open my suitcase.

Moments ago, the man at the X-ray machine had tapped my black hard-shell suitcase with a long stick to indicate the arrival of booty from overseas.

The moment the stick fell on my bag, I knew my Ardbeg was a lost cause. I would still go through my well-rehearsed 'shock and awe' tactics, and put up a brave defence. This was, after all, not the first time I was trying to smuggle alcohol into Pakistan. There was a small chance that I would still walk out of the airport with that alcohol bottle. I knew the drill only too well.

Luck plays a major role when you try to sneak liquor into Pakistan. During an earlier trip, I was crossing over to Pakistan via the Wagah–Attari border, and I had a bottle of Glenmorangie—the fruity Scottish single malt—in my bag. I decided to take advice from the friendly Pakistani porter, for a small extra fee. 'Inshallah,' he said, 'the X-ray machine won't work most probably, and your bottle will be safe.'

Alcohol is illegal in Pakistan. Well, mostly. The Zulfikar Ali Bhutto regime, under pressure from right-wing parties, had banned alcohol in the country way back in April 1977. For Bhutto it was a personal sacrifice. Earlier that year, Bhutto had publicly stated: '*Haan, mein sharab peeta hoon . . . laikan awam ka khoon nahi peeta!* [Yes, I drink, but I do not drink the people's blood].'

Not that Pakistanis don't drink. Many of them do, including 'good' Muslims. Many of my friends, 'good' and 'bad' Muslims, and non-Muslims, would often invite me to their evening parties. The big difference between drinking alcohol in India and Pakistan is the cheap thrill of risk-taking: the more secretive your booze party, the more fun it is.

In the snaky by-lanes of Lahore and Karachi, a bottle of whisky is not hard to find. If you are a non-Muslim, you can sign a permit and get drinks delivered to your hotel room, most likely by a non-Muslim man. At Lahore's Avari Hotel, I was served by a fellow Christian from Pakistan, who not only poured my drink but was keen to strike up a conversation about the difficulties of being a Christian in Pakistan. Russian vodka, European Scotch, home-brewed Murree beer— Pakistan has it all. I stay away from the local whisky, which looks more like dressed-up hooch. Hence the Ardbeg.

I decided to front-load the non-Muslim argument. I explained about my previous visits and how I'd been allowed to keep my bottle. 'You're a guest,' they had told me then. This guy was not interested in the least.

'Is this the only bottle in your suitcase?'

'*Chod deejiye, saab . . . Hum Dilli se aaye hai* [Let it go, saab . . . I've come from Delhi],' I told him in the typical South Asian way, subtly extolling the virtues of tolerance, and letting other people have their food (and drink) preferences.

'Oh, but I have already started filling the form.' He stopped scribbling, and looked up at me, feigning helplessness.

Was he angling for a small fee to let me have my bottle back? I wasn't sure but I was certainly not going to try and bribe a Pakistani customs official in Lahore. He took my bottle and gave me a recovery memo from the Office of the Superintendent of Customs, Allama Iqbal International Airport. So much for my smooth-talking abilities.

I would spend the next four days without any whisky. Well, except one evening, at the Kohsar Market. It's not that I can't do without it. Alcohol is like an alter ego, the smoother side of our selves. It's like transcendental meditation for dummies.

I had landed in Lahore less than an hour ago from Delhi in PK-271, a small ATR plane that took me on a bumpy ride. Pakistan International Airlines (PIA) is the only flight service available to travel from Delhi to Lahore if you do not want to cross by foot at the Wagah–Attari border. The visa was granted just one day before my flight.

For the agnostic in me, the PIA in-flight announcement over Lahore—'*Inshallah, hum jaldi Lahore utrenge* [God willing, we will land in Lahore shortly]'—was a bit bothersome. I wasn't sure if I wanted to leave it to God: I had a flight to catch for Islamabad.

'We have a roomful of bottles,' said the officer, unlocking the door behind him to show me rows of confiscated alcohol, arranged in no particular order and enough to keep a party going for months. 'We will eventually destroy them using a steamroller.' He was reassuring me that they were not for personal use but had been confiscated because it was the law of the land. That they would even confiscate bottles from the Americans and Chinese. Maybe he didn't want to be seen as inhospitable to Indians, or he was thinking of discounts in Chandni Chowk if he ever made it to India (he had seemed curious when I had said I was from Delhi). It didn't matter— by then I knew my Ardbeg wasn't making it out of the Lahore airport with me.

The E75 Expressway

I arrived at the Muzaffarabad brigade HQ one December evening last year in a Pakistan Army vehicle accompanied by a well-read colonel, a soft-spoken major, several army soldiers wearing Pathani suits and quite a few AK-47s. The colonel turned out to be a PhD candidate at Islamabad's Quaid-i-Azam University (QUA). We chatted away. The major and the AK-47s kept silent. The soldiers made sure to avoid eye contact. They would literally look away when I tried to catch their eye. This was a few hours before the colonel's shocking revelation about knowing all about me.

'My PhD defence is a week away,' the colonel, a man in his mid-forties, said.

'Great, let's discuss your findings.'

We hit it off in an instant. The colonel was to be my liaison officer (LO) during my stay in Pakistan—my first person of contact for anything I need and any clarification to be sought. He was tasked to be with me, watch me, check me out—throughout my stay. I was to be under his watchful eyes.

But he knew his job only too well. With his easy smile, he treated me like an old friend. He didn't make me feel out of place, was well read and had even published a couple of Urdu poetry books. What was a man of words doing in the Pakistani army?

He had received me at the Benazir Bhutto International Airport the previous evening and had taken me to Ambassador Aziz Ahmed Khan's home where I would be staying while I was in the Pakistani capital. The colonel left me at Aziz's drawing room, where he was waiting for my arrival.

The tall, elderly, ever-smiling and gracious Pathan gentleman is one of the nicest Pakistanis I know. Aziz and his wife Aisha were legendary hosts while they were in New

Delhi, and equally hospitable now in Islamabad in the prime of the former's retirement. I spent three evenings in their first-floor living room discussing their fond memories of India, political developments between the countries and how the two countries missed the bus on Kashmir.

'They were the good times,' Aziz muttered with a deep sense of nostalgia.

Their home is a mini-India, from a civilizational point of view. Statues and paintings from all over the country, Odisha to Kerala, line the muted walls and ledges. Aziz's basement has framed photos from his younger days on his old work desk—those of Rajiv Gandhi, Hilary Clinton and a host of other world leaders.

'I don't read newspapers,' he told me. 'I listen to the news or browse for news. I am growing old, you see.'

Aisha, an avid mountaineer and environmental activist, continues to be engaged in several developmental projects in Pakistan's far-flung areas. Their two sons are away in the US.

'My younger son, who is of your age, had a friend from Kerala,' Aziz once told me, mischievously. 'I secretly hoped that he was dating her!'

Aziz had given me my first-ever visa to Pakistan, thirteen years ago, when I used to be younger and far more adventurous. I had waited several hours outside the imposing gate of the Pakistan High Commission in Delhi's Chanakyapuri, talking on the phone to Aziz's secretary for my visa. I had then imagined Aziz to be a cold, hard-nosed Pakistani diplomat whose staff had made me wait outside the high commission for three hours. When I met him in 2008, I realized I had been completely off the mark. Aziz is a delightfully charming and wonderful man—and three hours is the quickest possible time to get a Pakistani visa, he assured me. Over the years, I have understood that he wasn't just smooth-talking.

Aziz sounds both bitter and sentimental when he talks about his stint in New Delhi as Pakistan's high commissioner (HC)—bitter because bilateral relations hit a roadblock in 2008 even though he left things in good shape in 2006. 'Between India and Pakistan, you can never be sure of what might happen tomorrow,' he would say. 'If only the leaderships showed a little more courage.'

Aziz was appointed HC by chance, just two months prior to his retirement from the Pakistan Foreign Service. In early May 2003, Riaz Khokhar, his Foreign Secretary, called Aziz to tell him that he was preparing a list of senior officers who could be considered for appointment as the envoy to India, a prestigious position for Pakistani diplomats. Khokhar also told him frankly that since Aziz had only a few months before retirement, he was unlikely to be considered for the post.

A few weeks later, in an interview, Saeed Naqvi, an eminent Indian journalist and columnist, asked the then Pakistani Prime Minister Mir Zafarullah Khan Jamali who was going to be sent to India as the high commissioner. Jamali quickly answered, 'Riaz Mohammad Khan.'

Rai Riaz, press secretary to Prime Minister Jamali, rushed to him soon after the interview and told him that it would be improper if an Indian media outlet were to announce Riaz's appointment before the Pakistani media did. So an interview with Pakistan's state-run PTV was quickly organized for Jamali in which he announced that Riaz Khan, Pakistan's ambassador to China, would be the new HC to India.

President Musharraf wasn't happy when this was brought to his attention. 'What will Beijing think if we pull out our ambassador to China and send him to New Delhi?' Riaz had been sent to Beijing just the previous year, and China and Pakistan share a close strategic partnership: One of Pakistan's former prime ministers Syed Yousaf Raza Gillani once famously eulogized the friendship as being 'higher than the mountains, deeper than the ocean, stronger than steel and sweeter than honey'.

Musharraf didn't want to upset Beijing and so overturned Jamali's decision. Aziz Ahmed Khan was the next name on the list, and he was asked to go to New Delhi. Aziz Khan would tell his friends that high commissioner to New Delhi was his dream job, and this was how he got it.

He would nostalgically smile whenever I reminded him of the grand entry that he had made to India when Aisha and he crossed over into India via the Wagah–Attari border in November 2003 as Pakistan's new envoy. It was a historic moment.

'The handsome and ever-smiling Aziz Khan and his beautiful wife,' I would say.

'Don't make fun of an old man,' he would respond.

A Pathan by ethnicity, Aziz was also ambassador to Afghanistan and was probably one of the last few people to have met Mullah Mohammed Omar, the supreme commander and spiritual leader of the Taliban, before he went into exile.

'No, we didn't create the Taliban; they came into being on their own. We developed relations after they became a force to reckon with,' he would say in response to my insinuations that the Taliban had started out as an outfit mostly comprising Pakistani flunkies.

He had arrived four days after the two sides had stopped firing on the border, and served till September 2006. The year before he arrived in India, there were close to 6000 instances of cross-border firing in Jammu and Kashmir (J&K). During his three years as the high commissioner, the total number was thirteen. This was arguably the most peaceful the relationship between the two nuclear-armed rivals had been in a long time.

Upon my return from the Pakistani side of the LoC, Aziz and Aisha asked me to join them at a private dinner at the high-end 'Table Talk' restaurant in Islamabad's Kohsar Market. Tucked away among government bungalows and foreign missions, Kohsar Market is an expensive shopping complex catering to foreigners and wealthy Pakistanis. Liberal and welcoming, the place draws happy youngsters and chilled-out older men and women to music and fancy lights. 'That's the Foreign Secretary's house,' said Aziz, pointing towards a barricaded bungalow on the opposite side of the market.

On our way to the first-floor restaurant, Aziz pointed to a spot near a tall tree by the pavement and said, 'And this is where poor Salmaan was shot.' He meant the former governor of Punjab Salmaan Taseer, who was shot dead seven years ago. His bodyguard, Mumtaz Qadri, pumped twenty-six bullets into him with a sub-machine gun for being critical of Pakistan's draconian blasphemy law. The killer was later hanged by the Pakistan government, and his supporters went on to build a shrine for him. Hundreds of thousands offer prayers at his shrine every year. Coming from a country where temples had been erected for Mahatma Gandhi's killer Nathuram Godse, the shrine for Qadri failed to shock me. Thankfully, there is no shrine on the thoroughfare in Kohsar Market where Taseer was shot, but well-meaning Pakistanis know the importance of people like Salmaan Taseer, and the barbarity of the blasphemy law. 'Salmaan Taseer is a blasphemer and this is the punishment for a blasphemer,' the assassin Qadri had said when arrested for Taseer's killing.

Aziz often sounded nostalgic about the Pakistan of Jinnah's dreams. Jinnah is passé in contemporary Pakistan. He belongs inside glass frames behind the desks of government officials, symbolically behind the present times—a lot like the fate of Gandhi in today's India.

We walked up to the restaurant, with Aziz struggling to climb the stairs after his knee-replacement surgery. There were several familiar faces at the restaurant, including Aziz's predecessor in India, Ashraf Jehangir Qazi. Not surprisingly, the unknown among them warmed up to me quite quickly—for the Pakistani liberal elite, India retains a certain charm. Some boasted of multi-entry visas to India, some about annual holidays in Goa. This was a microcosm of Pakistan's intellectual elite, a group that closely resembles New Delhi's intellectual elite. The difference is this: Pakistan's liberal elite loves India, while the Indian elite has become more and more dismissive of Pakistan of late. In Islamabad or Lahore, people are more likely to host Indians, to treat them well and be starry-eyed about India. A Pakistani, or the subject of Pakistan, is less likely to be treated similarly in India.

We chatted, drank and disagreed on Kashmir, but not when it came to the soulful *shayari* or poetry of Faiz Ahmed Faiz. Faiz had written movingly when India and Pakistan were partitioned.

> *Ye daagh ujala, ye shab gazeeda seher*
> *Wo intezaar tha jiska ye wo seher tau nahi*
> *Ye wo seher tau nahin, jis ki aarzu le kar*
> *Chaley the yaar ke mil jayegi kahin na kahin*
> *Falak ke dasht mein taaron ki aakhri manzil*
> *Kahin tau hoga shab-e sust mauj ka saahil*
> *Kahin tau ja ke rukega safeena-e gham-e dil.*

> This stained light, this night-bitten dawn;
> This is not that long-awaited daybreak;
> This is not the dawn in whose longing,
> We set out believing we would find, somewhere,

In heaven's wide void,
The stars' final resting place;
Somewhere the shore of night's slow-washing tide;
Somewhere, an anchor for the ship of heartache.

The following morning, Aziz took me out to the Jinnah market. We first did the mandatory scouting at the Saeed Book Bank, which has the latest Indian books on its shelves. Both Bollywood films and Indian books make their way to Pakistan. You can walk into a multiplex in Pakistan and catch the latest Salman Khan flick or buy the latest Indian bestseller from Saeed's. We managed to find a few gems in the old bookshops across the road from the Saeed Book Bank. A few swanky malls have come up in the vicinity, frequented by young Pakistanis and a growing number of Chinese.

It was in a cafe in one of those malls that I had planned to meet my young friends, some of Professor Sadia Tasleem's students from the QAU in Islamabad—we had been in touch via social media. Sadia teaches nuclear strategy to young Pakistanis at QAU and has been my friend for several years. We first met in San Diego, USA for a nuclear conference and in Pakistan thereafter. Though we taught our respective students how to use nuclear weapons to deter each other's countries, we both realized the importance of building peace.

QAU has always reminded me of New Delhi's Jawaharlal Nehru University (JNU)—it is Pakistan's best public university, liberal, a bit anti-establishment and certainly argumentative. Lots of open spaces and young minds willing to engage with you. Over cups of coffee at the ground floor cafe in the Jinnah market mall, it became increasingly clear to me that the dreams, desires and disappointments of these young

Pakistani students were much the same as those of my own students at JNU back in New Delhi. Students talked about their backgrounds, how those backgrounds held them back and how they were struggling to break the mould. None of them had ever been to India—but said they would like to, certainly to Mumbai, old Delhi and JNU. For this generation of Pakistanis, there is no nostalgia nor memories of Partition and the rest. They are proud Pakistanis, but also liberal individuals who wish to see peace and progress. And 'India' (thankfully the younger they get the fewer their references to 'Hindustan') is the big next-door neighbour with whom they believe there should be peace. They are as concerned about Kashmir as young Indians are concerned about Baluchistan. Perhaps a little more.

One of the students caught me looking curiously at the Chinese men and women passing by, chatting away in Mandarin. 'There are a lot of them here these days. There are shops catering exclusively to the Chinese expats here,' he informed me. China may be Pakistan's strongest strategic partner, but their people are alien to each other. Conversely, India may be Pakistan's biggest enemy, but their people couldn't be more similar.

* * *

'Please make sure our guest is given a good tour of the border,' Ambassador Aziz had told the colonel when we arrived at his house in Islamabad's I-8 sector.

'Sure sir,', said the colonel and handed me a typewritten postcard titled 'Visit Program', which summed up the itinerary for the next four days.

Officers from the Pakistani *fauj* or army arrived on time the following morning at our doorstep to pick me up and take me to the LoC. I took another thirty minutes: it was a cold December morning in foggy Islamabad and I am an academic, not used to following rigid timings. The men stood at Aziz's gate, in the December cold, waiting: armed and geared up for the long road ahead.

Under two hours on the scenic Islamabad–Murree–Muzaffarabad Expressway or the E75 Expressway takes you to Murree, one of Pakistan's oldest hill stations on the Pir Panjal Range. Narrow streets, fresh snow, busy shops, bustling crowds and traffic jams. I kept an eye out for Murree beer. No luck. The officers skirted my beer-related queries. The expressway is still under construction and passes through Bhara Kahu, the biggest Union council of the federal capital Islamabad, to reach Murree.

Someone in the entourage told me that the Indian High Commission in Pakistan continues to have a guest house in the hill station, reminiscent of the good times. Permission to visit the guest house is rarely given, even to senior high-commission officials.

It's another three hours via road to get to Muzaffarabad from Murree. The expressway ends somewhere close to Kohala, a small town on the river Jhelum. From Kohala we resumed our journey on the S-2 Strategic Highway to reach Muzaffarabad.

I kept asking the officers to help me get a local SIM card with data connectivity. I knew I was making life difficult for them. Every time I asked, the colonel would text someone and would say, 'I have reminded them.' Who's 'them'? I wondered. I was finally given a SIM card in Muzaffarabad, but the network was terrible. The closer we got to the LoC, the weaker the connection become. And then it simply vanished. Both sides were perhaps not too keen to have the locals talk to each other.

Puzzled Looks and AK-47s

When the colonel had come to pick me up from the Islamabad airport the previous evening, he didn't have his uniform on. That made me wonder if he was from the ISI—an organization that has come to assume a larger-than-life stature. But it turned out that he was from the Inter-Services Public Relations (ISPR), what some people in India refer to as the Pakistan Armed Forces' well-oiled propaganda machine.

'You won't get many opportunities to spend money,' he said, as I was looking for a currency exchange at the Islamabad airport. Changing currency would have been easier in Wagah. It is normal to find Pakistani money changers loitering around as soon as you cross into Pakistan. 'We can change Indian money,' they mutter furtively into your ears, though they are hardly discreet—they don't seem to care if anyone sees them going about their business. Their rate is usually more generous than the official rate, they spare you the paperwork and the whole process is way quicker. They also hand out numbers of their Indian counterparts who will change your money to Indian currency once you're back home. While the Indian nationalist screams seek to paint Pakistan as the enemy, bilateral cooperation takes on a different hue at the Wagah–Attari border—where good nature passes seamlessly from one side to the other. Look closely when you visit the Wagah–Attari border next time: you would find handshakes between soldiers on both sides, handshakes between porters and a general sense of friendliness, not while the beating the retreat ceremony is on though.

'I have to visit the Saeed Book Bank . . . I have a huge "to buy" list,' I said to the colonel. Returning with Pakistani books is a ritual for me. Buying books in Pakistan makes sense: it's hard to get Pakistani books in India and it's way cheaper there. But bringing books from Pakistan to India is not as easy as you might think, especially in these times.

It was mid-2016. I was returning home from Lahore, via Wagah–Attari by foot.

'What do you do in India?' the inquisitive customs official asked me at Attari, after I crossed into India.

'I am a JNU professor.'

He laughed hearing the acronym, and his colleagues joined in. I wasn't amused, nor provoked.

I didn't blame them. The Kanhaiya Kumar incident was still in the news, and people were still appalled at how 'anti-national' JNU was and how boys and girls in their 'late twenties' were still pursuing their studies in JNU using 'taxpayer money'.

'Are any of these books anti-national?' the officer asked, looking at the twenty-odd books I had picked up in Lahore. I wondered if he was taking a dig at me by mentioning the phrase 'anti-national', a phrase that had at that time unfortunately become synonymous with JNU. He seemed serious and was waiting for an answer.

'These books are written by Pakistanis, published by Pakistani publishers for the Pakistani readers . . . so I really can't certify how pro- or anti-India they are,' I replied. He understood what I was getting at. 'Well, you are a professor, you need your books . . . so take them.'

Sometimes a quick answer goes a long way.

I later figured out that his question about 'anti-national' books wasn't a rhetorical one. Apparently, there is a list against which customs officials are supposed to double-check the titles of imported books given that so many books are banned in India!

We travelled to Murree in two cars. The colonel and I were in the back seat, while the major sat in the front and occasionally asked the stocky army driver: 'Morale high *haina?*'

'*Ji*, saab,' he would reply quickly while keeping his eye on the road. The colonel and the driver were unarmed whereas the soldiers in the escort vehicle made no effort to conceal their guns, nor their puzzled looks.

The colonel was keen on discussing political theory and I was keen to get right to the point. 'So what kind of weapons do you guys use on the LoC?' Not that this was not known to a keen observer of the CFV but researchers like to hear it from the horse's mouth. So we started talking about weapons.

Direct weapons in use on the LoC include small arms, 300–500-metre rocket-propelled grenades, 800-metre recoilless rifles, etc. The indirect weapons include field, medium and heavy artillery and mortars. 82-mm mortar is one of the favourites. The Indian side uses 106-mm recoilless guns, 130-mm artillery guns, anti-aircraft guns, anti-tank guided missiles (ATGMs), rocket launchers and automatic grenade launchers.

'You should ask this question to the GOC when you meet him.' He meant the general officer commanding. One of the interesting things about military organizations is that the lower-ranking officers never give definite answers, always referring you to senior officers when you ask them a sensitive question. One way of getting around that is to keep referencing what their retired seniors have said. This tends to ease up the conversation.

The colonel took premature retirement from the Pakistan Army on 1 May 2018. He is more of an intellectual, a poet, a man of ideas. He was awarded a PhD degree by the QAU for his thesis entitled 'Regional and Global Implications of Pakistan–China Relations'. He currently hosts a talk show for a Pakistani TV channel.

The Homework

Writing on the causes of CFV is not an easy task. There is hardly any data and government sources usually keep mum or give out uninspiring information. The data released by the Indian and Pakistani sources don't, for instance, tell you when, where and why CFVs occurred. Without those details, the data is mostly sterile.

Doing fieldwork to generate data is even more cumbersome. Getting through to one's own side of the border is hard enough; accessing the other side of the border is well-nigh impossible. Until you make it happen.

I once asked a retired ISI chief, someone who has been making news both in India and Pakistan, General Asad Durrani, in the middle of a conversation in Bangkok, 'Have you ever been on our side of the LoC?' He paused for a few seconds and said in a serious tone, 'Not with a visa.' I hope he was being light-hearted. In my case, I had a visa and I am no spook.

By the time I managed to get to the Pakistani side of the Kashmir border, I had been working on the violent LoC in Kashmir for over two years. In these two years, I, along with my team of researchers, had managed to interview over ninety officials (mostly from the Indian and Pakistani militaries), many of whom were retired from active service.

At first, it wasn't easy to get through to people and organizations. I took the easy way out by making use of my 'connections' and friendships that I had made in the track-II world of Indo-Pak relations. By 2016, I was a twelve-year veteran in the track-II world, and that helped. Track-II meetings, usually organized in neutral countries, bring together interlocutors from nations in an adversarial relationship—India and Pakistan, in this case—to discuss contentious issues, especially when tensions run high and governments do not talk. While most of the participants are retired officials or politicians, a few academics like myself often join these efforts.

I began my investigations with Lieutenant General Syed Ata Hasnain, the highly regarded former commander of the Kashmir-based XV Corps of the Indian Army. Hasnain is a former GOC of the XV Corps (based in Srinagar) and XXI Corps (based in Bhopal) and was later the Military Secretary. His father, Major General Syed Mahdi Hasnain, was one of the few Muslim officers to have risen to the rank of general in the Indian Army. The general has kept himself busy despite retirement—as a strategic thinker, public speaker, columnist and TV commentator. Talkative, pleasant and insightful, Hasnain is a great conversationalist.

One afternoon, I caught up with him at Delhi's India International Centre to discuss why CFVs take place. I had known Hasnain from the Ottawa Dialogue on India–Pakistan Relations which meets thrice a year in Bangkok to discuss India–Pakistan military issues. I had also heard of his excellent work in the Kashmir valley. He started out describing how tactical factors often lead to firing, and for a civilian like myself listening to him on the nuances of army operations on the LoC was a great learning experience. 'You must travel to the LoC. There is only so much you can learn about operational aspects by sitting in Delhi,' he recommended. That afternoon in early 2016 was a major turning point—I decided to examine the causes and consequences of CFVs by actually going to the border areas.

I then got through to several retired Indian and Pakistan Army officers including General H.S. Panag who had led two of India's key army commands, the Central and the Northern; T.K. Sapru, former northern army commander;

Vinod Bhatia, former Indian director general of military operations (DGMO); Waheed Arshad, former Pakistani chief of general staff (CGS); Tariq Majid, retired chairman of the Pakistani Joint Chiefs of Staff Committee (CJCSC); and General Tariq Waseem Ghazi, former defence secretary of Pakistan, among many others.

Once you get referred to a senior general by his contemporary, access problems tend to disappear. And if you do your homework well, retired officers will happily engage in hours of conversation. There was also a constant attempt at process tracing or reverse engineering—to use several interviews to trace back to the origins of events, operations and the run-up to them.

The art of interviewing is all about asking the right questions, especially when dealing with retired military officials who were once in the thick of the action. Questions need to get to the heart of the matter but also take into account that one is dealing with individuals who cannot, and will not, tolerate sensitive questions. This careful balancing act is at the root of any great interview.

I was keen on getting into their world, the world of the men in uniform who fought each other and yet respected each other. It was a curious world, rife with breathtaking adventure, mind-blowing stories and unforgettable heroism. I loved it, and I was welcome.

For me, this was to be a long-term intellectual relationship, not a one-off book project. In this line of work, trust matters. And I had to earn the trust of two warring sides—easier said than done as India and Pakistan are of the 'either with us or against us' persuasion.

There exists, in my opinion, a disconcerting level of compartmentalization of expertise and domain knowledge in the government. Government, contrary to what many people assume, is not an omniscient monolith—more often than not one agency/department doesn't know about the work of others, and they hardly ever talk to each other.

Inter-agency coordination, in my experience, is often an exercise in skilfully dodging questions and hiding facts. Each agency/force/department works in its own silo, jealously guarding its interests and domain knowledge, and unwilling to share it with anyone else. The lessons from the age-old Indian parable of the blind men and the elephant (in this story of a group of blind men, who had never known what an elephant is, try to understand it by touching it. Each of them touches a different part of the elephant's body and describes the elephant differently based on their tactile experience. As a result, each of them understands and describes the elephant very differently) readily spring to mind here. The job of a serious researcher then is to break the interdepartmental/agency/force barrier and get a comprehensive picture. My objective was simple: get an all-inclusive picture from the Indian side through various forces and departments and then go to Pakistan and complete that picture.

In short, I was not a babe in the woods travelling in PoK surrounded by well-trained/briefed Pakistani army officers. I had had several hours of in-depth conversations with retired Pakistani army officers and serving and retired Indian officers. I had cross-checked my sources and information several times over. I had done my homework. But actually seeing what you have read about and heard of is a different experience. And it indeed was. It is one thing to hear stories about the LoC and it's a completely different ball game when you land up in the thick of things. You can taste the tension in the air.

The men I would be meeting with would know what and how much to tell me. My job was to stretch that limit.

And know when to rephrase my questions. As one Pakistani brigadier once told me, 'We all know how this game is played, don't we?' I kind of did.

'Welcome to HQ 12 Division, Sir'

A young girl, in a sunflower-yellow dress, looked down from a tiny window at the ruckus below. She seemed hesitant to display too much interest, but her curiosity got the better of her. The fresh snow had turned to slush, and our cars were stuck a hundred metres from our destination. The soldiers wanted to push the cars up, and they politely declined my offer to help—it wouldn't have made a difference anyway. The cars would not budge. We left them behind and got into a four-wheeler with snow chains for the last lap.

Did the young girl peeping out the window of the Murree garrison's family quarter know I was Indian? She didn't seem surprised at our plight; maybe she was used to slushy snow and the problems it brings. I waved at her with the unsure smile of a perfect stranger. She quickly withdrew from the window. Soldiers laughed at me being given the cold shoulder. She came back to the window, curious and amused, but refused to indulge me. She liked the attention but didn't want to give any. Or perhaps she was heeding the instruction young kids are given by their parents—don't trust strangers. Sometimes young nations are also told the same, and they grow up distrustful. Or she just had an 'attitude', just as nations do, sometimes.

The snow chains worked. Our car revved up the hill at full throttle. I waved at the young Pakistani girl once more. Even though the little girl refused to indulge me, I had managed to make the impersonal soldiers laugh and smile, even as they tried to avoid eye contact.

'Welcome to HQ 12 division, sir,' said the army major who received me at the entrance of the imposing building. He rubbed his palms to warm them before he shook my hand. Everyone looked friendly and hospitable, treating me as an important guest. To me, the only important thing was the visit itself. I inquired about Internet and the answer still was 'Please wait.' We walked up to the second floor to meet the man for whom I had come to Murree—the GOC of the Pakistan Army's 12 Infantry Division, also called the Chinar Division.

It was an unforgiving, cold winter forenoon. There was neither snow nor cold winds in Islamabad where we had started out that morning—the Murree garrison had both. Smartly uniformed army bearers kept bringing cups of green tea to the office of Colonel Waqas. Waqas was the colonel staff to the GOC, a powerful position since the selection is made from among the best colonels in the division. We were waiting to meet the GOC at this office overlooking the picturesque Murree hills. An easy smiler, Waqas beamed up and talked to me about my research and visit, in between the non-stop phone calls he was attending to. I was impressed by his ability to juggle tasks: talking to those present in his office, handling at least three landlines and a couple of cell phones, asking the bearers to bring green tea and biscuits.

He spoke into the phone, keeping the receiver close to his mouth, perhaps ensuring that I wouldn't overhear inputs coming from the various brigades of his boss's division posted on the LoC. 'First visit to Pakistan?' he asked, in between calls. Waqas is short, sturdy and alert and talks to everyone in his office in turn, while sitting on his chair from where he can occasionally sneak a look at the snow-clad Murree hills through the glass window. I like to think that the view is a constant reminder of nature's beautiful indifference to human conflict at the border. The wall behind him was adorned by the framed pictures of the President, prime minister and army chief. There were miniature weapons and framed photographs on the table—everything in his office seemed to be in military precision despite it being an exceptionally busy establishment.

'No, I have been to Pakistan several times before,' I replied.

He looked surprised. 'You should visit India,' I said, and both of us laughed loudly, along with the others in the room. 'Hopefully not atop a tank,' I added to the welcome mirth.

The 12 Infantry Division's GOC, for whom I was waiting, had to be among the Pakistan Army's best major generals, not just because the division mans the crucial LoC in northern and central Kashmir but also because it is Pakistan's largest infantry formation: 6 infantry brigades, 1 divisional artillery brigade and a number of air defence units, among others. The division, formed in 1948, had played a crucial role in all the three major India–Pakistan wars: 1947–48, 1965 and 1971.

The 12 division of the Pakistan Army was raised in 1948 in Peshawar and moved to the more serene Murree hills two years later—it has been headquartered there since. The division often finds mention in Indian newspapers for firing on the LoC and aiding terrorist infiltrations into the Indian side of Jammu and Kashmir. Most recently, the Indian Army claimed that its Ghatak Commandos had carried out a cross-LoC operation and killed soldiers of the 59 Baloch regiment of the 12 division. This was only twelve days after I returned from the Murree Cantonment.

The '(In)famous' Dinner Party

When the invitation from the Pakistan Army finally came through in mid-December 2017, a certain dinner party at Mani Shankar Aiyar's house, where the Gujarat elections were allegedly 'rigged', was dominating the news in New Delhi. There were fiery debates in TV studios, with the BJP leaders highlighting the impropriety of the dinner, and the Congress party defending the attendees at the dinner. Like a number of faux political issues, it was both ominous and silly.

While on the election trail in the Banaskantha district of Gujarat, Prime Minister Narendra Modi had alluded to a 'conspiracy' that was 'hatched' at Aiyar's house in Delhi: 'A Pakistan delegation meets at Mani Shankar's house and the next day he disrespects Gujarat's society, its *pachat* (backward) society, its poor and Modi. Don't all these things raise questions and concern?'[1]

He didn't stop at that. 'Aiyar held a meeting for three hours, and then the next day, Mani Shankar calls Modi "*neech*". This is a serious and sensitive issue. Also, what is the reason for such a secret meeting amidst Gujarat elections?'[2]

Former prime minister Manmohan Singh had also attended the dinner. He was deeply upset by these remarks and later came out with a stinging rebuttal of Modi's insinuations. 'PM Modi must apologize to nation to restore dignity of his office,' he demanded.[3]

Aiyar is not some ordinary leader of the Congress party. A seasoned politician and a confidant of former prime minister Rajiv Gandhi, Aiyar had taken voluntary retirement from the Indian Foreign Service to join the Gandhi cabinet, and was most recently a member of the Manmohan Singh cabinet.

A well-read intellectual, he never minces his words. Some say he is intellectually arrogant,[4] but a more accurate characterization is that he doesn't tolerate stupidity. Aiyar's columns often spark controversies, as do his public utterances. And Modi is known to milk Aiyar's bold but ill-timed words to his political advantage.

During the high-voltage 2014 election campaign which eventually propelled Modi into the prime minister's seat, Aiyar had, for instance, said, 'I promise you in 21st century Narendra Modi will never become the Prime Minister of the country . . . But if he wants to distribute tea here, we will find a place for him.'[5] Modi's party, the BJP, lost not one moment in cashing in on Aiyar's comment. They launched the '*Chai pe charcha* with NaMo' campaign. Modi's BJP went on to crush the Congress party in the 2014 elections.

And now, just a week before my visit to Pakistan was to materialize, Modi had basically accused Aiyar, a former federal minister (and a former two-tenure prime minister of the country, Manmohan Singh) of having colluded with the Pakistanis to conspire against him. Now that's a serious charge, notwithstanding the purely electoral intent behind it (the 'conspiracy at Aiyar's house' did not survive the Gujarat elections though).

I would not have thought twice about going on a field trip to Pakistan—that's what I wanted to do for a long time and it is what I do as a researcher. But this time was different. I was to go to Pakistan during a live, high-voltage Indian election campaign with Pakistan's name taken in political rallies by the ruling party.

The BJP and its social media army was upping the ante. It accused Congress of crossing the 'national line on Pakistan'. Not that anyone had delineated a line on Pakistan but like many things in India, there was always an assumed line. One of the BJP's ideologues wrote in the media: 'Manmohan Singh's Dinner with Pakistanis Is Unforgivable'.[6]

The Congress party hit back: 'The PM made a stopover in Pakistan to attend a marriage ceremony in PM Nawaz Sharif's family. Was he invited there?'[7]

These were bad times for Indo-Pak relations.

Would accepting an invite from the Pakistan Army and visiting PoK amount to me crossing the 'national line on Pakistan', as the BJP had accused Aiyar of? Not that they had spelt out the dos and don'ts that could define such a policy. In the current atmosphere where sedition charges are tossed like Frisbees by politicians, a normal visit like mine could easily end up being twisted into something labelled 'anti-national'.

I have always believed that when in doubt, it's best to talk to others. I reached out to my friends and colleagues. The cautious ones among them advised me to be careful. What if someone in the BJP makes an issue of a JNU professor's visit to PoK as a guest of the Pakistan Army? What if one of those anti-JNU pro-BJP news channels carries a ticker about my 'disgraceful' violation of the national policy on Pakistan?

I was often accused of organizing and participating in track-II events with Pakistanis during times of heightened bilateral tension: 'How can Indians participate in track-II events organized in fancy five-star hotels when our soldiers are getting killed on the LoC?' some among the Twitterati would angrily quip.

What if some nondescript *sena* or group decided to blacken my face?

Despite being awarded the best university in the country, year after year, JNU is the Indian right's bête noire. And JNU professors are suspect to begin with. In early 2016, the Indian home minister Rajnath Singh claimed that 'The nation must accept the reality that the incident that took place in JNU had the backing of LeT chief Hafiz Saeed. This is unfortunate.' That he was referring to a tweet from a fake handle attributed to a Pakistan-based terrorist was a matter of detail which not many people bothered themselves with.

I had made my own life difficult over the years, by being vocal and critical in my columns in *The Hindu*. I tell it like it is, and I see no way around the facts.

Then there were the adventurous friends. 'You are neither breaking any law nor are you doing anything illegal by going there. Moreover, you are a writer who would write about it. If you have something to hide, you wouldn't write about it, right?' That's exactly what I did when I returned. I wrote a column in *The Hindu* announcing the details of my 'anti-national' act.

In my line of work, secrecy is a liability.

Many years ago, I was asked by Pentagon officials to give a briefing to officers of the United States Pacific Command. I asked a colleague for his opinion. 'Do you know anything you are not supposed to know?' he asked. 'I don't even know what I am supposed to know,' I responded.

That's my approach to national security: I don't want to know what I am not supposed to know. But then how do I know what it is that I am not supposed to know?

It had taken Rawalpindi, also called 'Pindi', around one and a half years to process my request and 'check me out'. I had waited far too long for this. There was no way I was letting go of this opportunity. I drove to the Pakistan High Commission in Chanakyapuri, Delhi, that afternoon to get my passport stamped by the visa counsellor. The visa section was generous this time around. A year ago I had only received a single-city visa, but now I was given a visa which could take me to Lahore, Islamabad, Rawalpindi and all of PoK—thanks to the Pakistan Army. This was a coup (no pun intended!).

The Chain-Smoking General

Colonel Waqas ended the call, wore his cap, stood up and turned to me: 'Sir, the general is ready to meet you now.' The characteristic smile had disappeared from his face. He looked serious and formal now, as if preparing for something that required a certain amount of decorum.

I was busy chatting with his colleagues: young, courteous officers of the Pakistan Army. The conversation almost never went beyond the very basic—they very well knew how, and how much, to talk to someone from the 'enemy' country. Most of them were probably seeing an Indian for the very first time in their life, except of course through the lens of their telescopic guns on the LoC.

I walked into the room next door, accompanied by Waqas and his colleagues. As we entered the large, imposing corner office with an abundance of natural light, the officers stood upright and saluted an unsmiling man with a lampshade moustache. The general gestured his subordinates to ease but they continued to stand at attention. A heady cloud of power, and cigarette smoke, hung heavy in the presence of the major general. The room smelt of bittersweet tobacco and burnt coffee. There was miniature weaponry on the table, a large chandelier hanging from the tall ceiling, and swords and guns decorating the wall along with framed pictures of men in uniform, and one without it, Quaid-i-Azam Muhammad Ali Jinnah. The tall man extended his hand, staring unblinkingly at me.

Major General Azhar Abbas, the Murree-based 12 Infantry Division's GOC, is an impressive man: tall, sharp-looking, chain-smoking with a firm handshake. He is a complete contrast to his colonel staff. He doesn't smile easily, and during the one and a half hours I spent in his office, he almost never did. 'You may now leave,' he ordered his men after the photographers had finished recording the enemy presence in the GOC's chamber. 'You may already know about me,' he said. He had expected me to do my homework. Thankfully, he introduced himself, talking about his past appointments, family, current engagements, etc. That was a short-lived warm moment in an otherwise serious encounter.

'Mind if I smoke?' he asked me—and didn't wait for my answer. He took out a cigarette from the pack, flicked his lighter, inhaled and held the smoke in, all in one fluid movement. All the while he kept looking at me. Of course, I was not going to tell him that cigarette smoke gives me a headache. The trade-off between an interview with the general manning the LoC with India, and shelling it periodically, for a smoke-induced headache didn't seem unreasonable.

'I have read it,' he said when I gave him a copy of my paper on the causes of CFVs. 'I partly agree with you on the local military factors triggering CFVs', he said, 'but there's more. The story is complicated.'

In my writings, one of the key arguments I make about what causes CFVs on the J&K borders is that local military factors often trigger violence—these include operations to 'test the new boys' when new units get posted to an area, the personality traits of local commanders, a lack of standard operating procedures, etc.

'There was a time (for instance, during 2002) when troops had a great deal of liberty with regard to firing, but not any more. They are a disciplined lot today,' he pointed out.

'Political factors,' he said, 'are a major cause of CFVs these days. It's government policy, not decided by local chaps.' He was keen to stress upon the problems faced by the Pakistani side given how civilians lived very close to the zero line, unlike on the Indian side.

'Sometimes the terrain can be so disorienting that civilians might lose their way and cross the line, triggering firing by the Indian side,' he said.

'Well, it's the Indian side that undertakes operations by Border Action Teams (BATs) on our side, we don't,' he said, cutting me off when I mentioned how Pakistani BATs are said to have created a lot of instability on the LoC.

'Of course not, we don't send any terrorists into your side,' he said, firmly pushing back when I asked whether covering fire leads to CFVs. I left it at that.

'How about withdrawing heavy artillery to 40 kilometres behind the zero line to avoid escalation of violence?' I asked him.

'It must be 50 kilometres since the range of many of these high-calibre weapons is 40 kilometres, but it's a good idea. Is there any appetite for it in your country?' he responded.

Now that was a great suggestion for a potential confidence-building measure between the two forces. The first step towards calming the border is to lower the calibre of firing. I would flag this suggestion at several levels upon my return to New Delhi.

It was time to say goodbye to the general. Here was a man who was manning one of the most challenging and sensitive conflict areas in South Asia. It was not difficult to understand why he was a commanding figure. I still keep the 12 division memento that the GOC presented to me at the end of our conversation on behalf of the 'GOC & ALL RANKS 12 DIV'. This piece of 'enemy property' has its own corner at my home in New Delhi.

'*Semper est paratum*' (Latin for 'always ready') is the credo of the Chinar Division of the Pakistan Army. The Indian Army's XV Corps based in Srinagar is also called 'Chinar'—Chinar Corps, which faces Pakistan's 12 Infantry Division in Kashmir. Chinar is also symbolic of the rich Kashmiri heritage.

The general pressed the bell; Waqas returned to the room and stood still after a salute. 'Call the colonel,' the general said. The colonel arrived soon thereafter. 'I am now leaving the professor in your care. Make sure he gets a good view of the LoC and take care of him. Colonel Staff has instructed my men in the forward areas. They know what to do,' he told the colonel.

'Call me if you need anything,' said the general and turned to me, extending his hand again. 'He will look after you.'

Knowledge—listening to and learning from your 'enemy'— makes you humble and human. I was getting comfortable with the ways and customs of the enemy forces. And my journey inside the enemy territory had only just begun.

The Men Who Took Me to the Enemy Territory

The Vasant Vihar Man

As I was parking my car in Vasant Vihar, south Delhi's posh neighbourhood, I noticed a man nonchalantly jotting down my car's registration number. He had on a safari suit that made him stand out like a sore thumb and he wasn't bothered that I had noticed him. Staring at him didn't make a difference, as was expected given where I was and who I was about to meet. I didn't know the man, but I knew it was his business to do exactly what he was doing. So I flashed him a knowing smile and confidently went up to the gate of the two-storey building in front of me. He stared at me expressionlessly, a tad bored. He probably knew that I knew who he was—a faceless minder on a routine surveillance mission.

This is something one gets used to in the whole India–Pakistan business. I was there to meet a certain official from the Pakistan High Commission whose report could make or break my journey to Pakistan. Someone came out of the house, opened the gate, observed the surroundings, ignored the man standing at a distance and invited me inside.

'Why do you want to visit our side of the Line of Control?' the Vasant Vihar man asked me as we sat down to speak. Before that he had courteously asked if he could keep my phone at a distance. 'Hope you understand—please don't mind.' I didn't have an issue with that; I wasn't going to record him. He was a serving officer; he had his worries. How was he going to trust an Indian whom he had only heard about? Sure, it was his home, but it was still India, his enemy country. He asked me to keep my phone in flight mode, under a cushion, at the far end of the living room.

Next time I met him, it was at a private club belonging to a Western embassy, reserved strictly for members. Again he asked me to switch to flight mode and kept looking at the screen as I did the needful. Call it paranoia, but this man did not want to take any chances.

I was there to explain my intention to visit PoK: to convince him that I had nothing but purely academic interests in going to PoK. It's funny how we had to converse using mismatched terminologies: he would refer to Azad Jammu and Kashmir (AJK) and India-occupied Kashmir (IoK) and I would refer to PoK and J&K. But we understood each other perfectly well. These terms came to us naturally, stemming straight from our 'national lines' vis-à-vis each other. Neither of us minded it.

For the next two hours, I was left without the personal care of my most trusted companion. It's surprising, and a little unnerving, how mobile phones have come to occupy such intimate and omniscient personal spaces in our lives.

There was a reason why the Vasant Vihar man was asking 'why'. The book I was writing about CFVs in J&K required a visit to the Pakistani side of the LoC, and my request for doing so was still under review by the higher echelons of the Pakistan Army in Rawalpindi. Even though they took close to eighteen months, they went about their assessment methodically. I assumed this member of the Pakistan High Commission was conducting a live interview to see if I checked out.

He wanted to know the source of my interest (or 'angle'). I replied I was doing it in my national interest. He looked curious, so I explained, 'I am convinced that it is in my national interest that India and Pakistan make peace, and I am contributing whatever little I can.'

'National interest' is a complicated business—because it has no content to it. It's an empty but extraordinarily powerful phrase which can be invoked by interested parties at any given point of time, depending on what they need to justify. 'National interest' as a concept does not change, but its contents are subject to a variety of factors. You can justify almost anything using 'national interest', and that is the scary part. At the same time it's liberating, because 'national interest' is not just the monopoly of a few people, namely those in power. I can decide whether what I do and how I do it is in consonance with national interest—as I see it, of course.

'I have been asked to give an opinion about you. You see, in matters such as this, no one wants to take a chance recommending that we invite an Indian to a sensitive area— keep him in our mess, let him mingle with our officers and men, and take him to the live LoC, etc. It's tricky and no one really wants to take that responsibility,' he told me.

He was right. I was on a no-entry list (more on that later), and it would take a highly placed Pakistani official to get me off that list. My colleagues from the various track-II dialogues were helping me get an invite from Rawalpindi, but it would take a serving officer to fix the problem at the end of the day. It had to be an inside job.

He was the man who could do it, and I was sitting in his basement drawing room. This was the moment, and I had to convince him. My life's most serious research journey hinged on this man's assessment of me. It was the kind of opportunity you chase after like a child after a will-o'-the-wisp. Such chances don't simply come by; you have to make them happen. He had done his homework and had read a great deal of my writing. There were almost no serious gaps in his knowledge about me: he knew about my activism, political views and social background. He even quoted directly from my writings: 'I really liked what you wrote about the Wagah flag ceremony—"choreographed hostility".' He was referring to an article that Kaveri Bedi and I had written for *The Hindu* on the mindlessness of the Wagah ceremony.[1] 'And I agree with you, it must be stopped.'

I was surprised by this. He actually agreed with me? Was this some kind of a test? I had heard that one way of 'getting through to your subject' is by agreeing with him—some sort of reverse psychology which puts the subject at ease, and exactly at that 'lowering-of-the-guard' moment you can find his soft spot. Was he smooth-talking me? Trying to turn me? Turn me how? For what? At a moment like that, I couldn't help but overthink it all.

We talked for over two hours—about Kerala, LoC, JNU politics and, of course, the Pakistan Army. I was in a bit of a hurry. I had literally been packing my bags when he called me the previous evening for a meeting. I had a flight to catch for Bangkok in the next four hours. I quickly finished the sumptuous breakfast he offered and drove back home.

He had checked me out. He seemed positive and convinced. But then appearances can be deceptive, especially in this game. People are trained to be deceptive; they get paid for it. Deception is a carefully cultivated industry in the business of statecraft.

'Rest assured I will give a positive report. I am convinced your visit will be useful for all parties. But please do note that there are several organizations involved in this sort of business and each will have their own views about things. It is hard to overrule concerns especially when you are on a no-entry list,' he said.

He then walked with me to see me off. While we were still at the gate, a white Maruti Gypsy sped past, the men inside looking intently at us. One of them was the man in the safari suit.

Why was I on a no-entry list? Did they think I was some kind of a double agent or something? What would happen to my future research on Pakistan if they denied me a visa this time, despite the attempts of the powerful man I had just had breakfast with? These questions kept bothering me on my way home, all the way to the airport and finally in Bangkok that evening. I didn't want to delve into that question then, nor did I have the time. So I decided to take it up when I got back.

The Vasant Vihar man kept his word. He drafted a positive report stating why I should be given a visa and allowed a visit. And he lobbied for it. I know this because the invitation from Rawalpindi eventually came through.

Ghazi, the Hard Hitter

'I have seen Pakistani army posts at less than 50 metres from our side of the LoC. Since then I have had an irresistible desire to see the Indian Army posts from your side of the LoC,' I told Lieutenant General Tariq Waseem Ghazi (retired) in March 2016.

'What are you up to, my friend?' he said with a laugh, amused at first. You can't blame him. This was an unusual request. Ghazi laughs loudly, talks tough and is a hard hitter. But more importantly, he is a friend of friends.

Except for the infiltrating militants/terrorists, and Indian and Pakistani troops who carry out cross-border operations (à la 'surgical strikes'), no one really manages to be on both sides of the LoC. But those creeping through in the dead of night don't need a visa. I would. More so, I wasn't up to anything clandestine, though I did crave the occasional adventure.

In India, Ghazi is viewed as a hardliner, an India-hater and a puritan on Kashmir. That is the conventional wisdom about him. A teetotaller like a number of his Pakistan Army contemporaries, Ghazi had missed his chance to become Pakistan's chairman of the Joint Chiefs of Staff Committee. The then president/army chief made Ghazi's junior, and Musharraf's protégé, Ehsan ul-Haq, the CJCSC in October 2004. When superseded, seniors resign—that's the tradition. Ghazi followed the tradition in letter if not in spirit. His resignation letter had reached the Military Secretary's table within an hour of his supersession, but he wasn't too happy about it. He had kept it ready, as the rumours had reached him well before the event. Musharraf had decided to appoint Haq in place of Ghazi. Many believed this was because the latter was thought to be less of a 'yes man', and the military dictator didn't want to take a chance with Ghazi.

Musharraf made up for it later by making Ghazi the country's Defence Secretary. 'Tariq, what do you want me to do for you?' he asked Ghazi when he met him for a courtesy call after the lieutenant general's resignation.

'Nothing, sir, I have returned home.'

'But I am not ready to let you go . . . Why don't you take over as Defence Secretary after Hamid [Lieutenant General Hamid Nawaz Khan] completes his term in May next year?' Ghazi and his wife Afshan had already shifted to Karachi so that Ghazi could go back to his old hobbies: boating, and maintaining his vintage car collection. But he didn't decline Musharraf's offer. For a retired Pakistani general, the job of a powerful Defence Secretary can be very attractive.

'Frankly, I was excited when Musharraf offered me the job. I had no such expectations when I walked into the army house to meet him,' Ghazi told me later.

In the meantime, the rivalry between Ghazi and Haq continued. Later in 2006, when Musharraf decided to take military action against the popular Baloch leader Nawab Akbar Shahbaz Khan Bugti, Ghazi, in his capacity as the Defence Secretary, advised the former to negotiate with the septuagenarian leader. The two were at loggerheads, especially after rockets were fired in Kohlu during Musharraf's visit to Baluchistan on 14 December 2005. Ghazi continued with his efforts to ensure Bugti was spared Musharraf's wrath.

But Haq and his former organization, the ISI, weren't happy about it and torpedoed his suggestion for a diplomatic overture towards Bugti. Haq advised Musharraf against negotiating with Bugti and eventually prevailed. Bugti was killed by the Pakistan Army under the orders of Musharraf. 'It shouldn't have been done, but Musharraf listened to Ehsan rather than me. I had organized a meeting between Bugti and Musharraf and even sent a helicopter to fetch Bugti to Islamabad. I was overruled and the pilot was asked to return without Bugti on board,' Ghazi recalls. ISI's machinations killed Bugti, and Musharraf continues to fight the case against him in Pakistani courts.

When Ghazi was called out of retirement to head the defence ministry in Islamabad, he was busy refurbishing and tending to his vintage car collection in Karachi, in particular the 1934 Ford V8 Roadster, as well as managing an army farm in the heart of Karachi. He would make daily rounds of the farm to speak to the tenants who were taking care of it. He was getting comfortable as a retiree when he was asked to head back to Islamabad.

One of his immediate assignments was to continue talks on Siachen with the Indian side. This was during the heyday of Indo-Pak relations, and Musharraf wanted to make a difference and was serious about his peace overtures. When the talks were looking up, Ghazi asked Musharraf what his instructions were. 'I want a resolution to Siachen. I am looking at a potential resolution of the Kashmir dispute in 2007 and that is a big-ticket item for me.'

'On whose terms?' Ghazi asked Musharraf.

'See, now you are complicating it. *Pasoodi mat dalna* [Don't put a spanner in the works], Tariq, resolve it. No diplomatic language, nitpicking over commas . . . Resolve it as best as you can. Talk to the Indians. I need this done.'

Musharraf knew only too well that Ghazi was a hardliner, but a highly competent hardliner. They would often exchange views on several things. They once talked about the botched-up Kargil operation of the Pakistan Army. Musharraf told Ghazi about a conversation with Nawaz Sharif. In March 1999, a couple of months after the Kargil operation had been launched, Sharif interrupted Musharraf's brief and asked, '*General sahib, Srinagar kab pahunchenge*? [General sahib, when will you reach Srinagar?]' Ghazi was sure Musharraf wasn't lying because he had heard the same story from another person who had been at the 1999 meeting.

Ghazi personally thinks that Kargil was initiated without the Nawaz Sharif–led civilian government's authorization (or even the authorization of the military establishment outside of the small coterie around Musharraf that dreamt it up). It was later endorsed by Sharif when it was presented to him as a fait accompli. Ghazi thinks it was a comedy of errors—a limited tactical move, spurred on by local and personal ambitions, which snowballed into an unintended and unplanned strategic provocation, something the military leadership suddenly found as being untenable. The cover-up of and lack of discussion on Kargil on the Pakistani side is proof of it being considered an embarrassing episode.

* * *

Despite his best efforts, Ghazi recalls, no headway could be made on Siachen. Or rather, some headway was made, but it didn't reach its logical conclusion.

In May 2005, a meeting between the two defence secretaries—Tariq Ghazi and Ajai Vikram Singh—took place at the Ministry of Defence in Rawalpindi. Ghazi urged the Indian delegation to treat the 1989 Rajiv–Bhutto statement as a starting point for discussions.[2] 'That time has passed,' the Indian delegation responded. The Indian line on Siachen had become harder. In 2004, India was more amenable to the authentication of existing troop deployments and then mutual withdrawal. It was Pakistan that had trouble with the term 'authentication' then.

According to Ghazi, while the Indian side was insisting on 'authenticating the current line' the Pakistani side wanted to know what came after the authentication—a question to which, Ghazi argues, there was no answer from the Indian delegation. 'Authenticating the line' is a process whereby the two sides identify their current locations on a map, exchange the maps and get each other's acknowledgement about the present deployment. Once they have acknowledged each other's current locations, they agree to withdraw to pre-decided locations behind the forward lines. Indians wanted the authentication to be done so that once the withdrawal took place, the Pakistani side would not occupy the positions vacated by India.

In another meeting in 2007 between the defence secretaries—Ghazi and his new Indian counterpart Shekhar

Dutt—Ghazi recalls having offered the Indian side that 'Pakistan will authenticate the AGPL [Actual Ground Position Line] but it is not a precondition but a part and parcel of the whole package of the whole set of agreements that we make,' and that issues such as 'withdrawal of forces, verification, monitoring, relocation, decision on where the relocation will take place, guarantee that nobody would violate, penalties applicable and the exchange of maps that laid out a movement plan from existing positions to projected positions, indications on exactly which weapon will move from where, what routes, what timings, etc.' would be part of the deal.

The Indian response to Pakistan's detailed Siachen proposal, according to Ghazi, continued to be the old one: only after authentication could other issues be discussed. Writings by the retired Indian officials substantiate Ghazi's argument.

In his book *How India Sees the World: Kautilya to the 21st Century*,[3] former Indian foreign secretary Shyam Saran writes that

> When the CCS meeting was held on the eve of the defence secretary–level talks (in 2006), [National Security Adviser M.K.] Narayanan launched into a bitter offensive against the proposal, saying that Pakistan could not be trusted, that there would be political and public opposition to any such initiative and that India's military position in the northern sector vis-à-vis both Pakistan and China would be compromised. [The then army chief Gen.] J.J. Singh, who had happily gone along with the proposal in its earlier iterations, now decided to join Narayanan in rubbishing it.

Saran was referring to the solution wherein the AGPL would be authenticated and an annexure would be signed with maps, marking the locations where Indian and Pakistani troops held positions prior to withdrawal.

In 2006, during a meeting that Ghazi had with Prime Minister Manmohan Singh in New Delhi, the latter advised him to call on M.K. Narayanan, which he did. Ghazi says he went over to Narayanan's office to reason with him on the mutual withdrawal issue.

But Narayanan, according to Ghazi, was not too keen on an Indian withdrawal from Siachen and was stuck on cross-border infiltration. 'We can't trust you on cross-border infiltration,' Narayanan told Ghazi bluntly. India's thinking and its position on Siachen had undergone a major change between 2004 and 2006—M.K. Narayanan seemed to have played a role in effecting this change. Ghazi returned to Islamabad empty-handed and his Siachen 'adventure' faded into the fog.

Ghazi doesn't mince his words. I was keen on getting him to India to have him talk to the strategic community in the country. I thought he was suitable for certain kinds of listeners in New Delhi who are used to straight-talking people who do not sugar-coat their views. And yet I knew that Ghazi's straight-shooting style might not be palatable for everyone, especially for the uninitiated. It was for this reason that I later requested him to talk about climate change—and thus steer clear of more sensitive topics—when he was addressing students at the South Asian University in New Delhi in February 2016—I didn't want anything to go wrong. I had deliberately left out JNU. Tirades against 'anti-national' elements in the country were on the rise those days. JNU was the prime target of right-wing trolling, and I too had been tagged 'anti-national' on occasion. Of course, I did tell Ghazi to speak his mind when addressing the strategic crowd behind closed doors; they were trained and knew enough of the backstory to be able to look beyond the narrow nationalist blinkers.

I lobbied for his visa with the authorities in New Delhi, as did several of my colleagues from our military-to-military track-II fraternity from the Ottawa Dialogue. My more experienced track-II colleagues agreed that despite his strong views, delivered equally strongly, Ghazi is a delightful man to chat with to get a feel of the temperature in Rawalpindi. In New Delhi, colleagues from the Ottawa Dialogue hosted him at the Gymkhana Club one evening. Ghazi is the quintessential party man who doesn't drink. I was surprised when almost every member of the track-II community turned up, and more.

'Why Tariq Ghazi? You know his views,' said some people in Delhi's bureaucratic circles, frowning, especially those in service or the newly retired.

'Because he will tell it like it is, without sweet-talking, and the man has a channel to the new bosses in Pindi,' I responded.

In several track-II conversations Ghazi had indicated that the army chief Qamar Javed Bajwa was keen on a rapprochement with India. Bajwa, Ghazi said, had asked to convey the idea that were there to be a rapprochement between Modi and Nawaz Sharif, Rawalpindi would not oppose it. It might seem like old news now, but not when Ghazi had conveyed it.

His visa was approved in less than a week in February 2016; as a matter of fact, his wife's visa took more time to process. The deep state in India certainly knows who to listen to in Pakistan.

* * *

'Ghazi sahab, I am serious. I want to visit your side of the LoC,' I said. We were travelling from the Hyatt Regency at Bhikaji Cama Place to the Observer Research Foundation (ORF), Delhi, where he would speak that morning to a packed audience on 'India–Pakistan Relations: Prospects and Challenges'. At ORF, he maintained his hard-line position, true to his reputation. Yet he answered each and every question from the audience, which consisted of retired bureaucrats, generals, members of think tanks, serving officials and soft-spoken spooks who never carry visiting cards.

I had known Ghazi since 2010 or so, when we began attending the Ottawa and Chao Phraya track-II dialogues. I was impressed with how organized he was. He routinely carried a black folder with a notepad inside to make detailed notes of what everyone around the table said. 'I refer back to it to refresh what people have said on earlier occasions, and it generally keeps my mind organized,' he said when I made fun of what I called his 'staff-officer style' of note-taking. He would use a pencil to scribble, shake his head in disagreement on hearing something he didn't like, smile mischievously when Indians took a dig at him, and spoke in a measured voice.

'If you are serious about it, we can give it a try. No guarantees, you know how these things are. But of course, it will take some time.' Our brief discussion on a visit to PoK ended there.

It was not an offhand request. I had been thinking about it for a long time. And I was determined to pursue it. Writing a book on the LoC based purely on visits to one side would be incomplete from a methodological point of view. By then, travelling along the borders and talking to the men in uniform had become more than an academic interest for me. I was getting passionately interested in it.

I hate wars and bloodshed, but the valour, sense of honour and the clarity of thought of the men in uniform— on both sides—fascinated me. To someone who spent several years of his teenage and early adulthood with Jesuit priests, training to think clearly, meditate deeply and imbibe a sense of honour, the armies of India and Pakistan were irresistibly appealing as objects of inquiry. I sensed an immediate connect with them.

It was early November 2016 when I reminded Ghazi about my request. We were in Bangkok for the Ottawa Dialogue, at the Shangri-La Hotel, on the bank of the Chao Phraya river. Several track-II dialogues take place in Bangkok. In fact, even the Indian and Pakistani national security advisers— Ajit Doval and Nasser Khan Janjua—have their off-the-radar dialogue in Bangkok as well. The Thai visa is easy to get; upmarket hotels are available at cheaper rates and it's faster to get there. The Thais are hospitable; more importantly, it's neutral ground to organize things that you do not want the media to push itself into.

At the Shangri-La, Ghazi and I were discussing the triggers of the recurrent CFVs on the LoC in Kashmir. This time General Ghazi's response was more serious: 'I will talk to the people concerned. Give me some time and you will definitely hear from me.' I did not hear from him for over two months.

But he kept his word. In March 2017, Ghazi wrote to me asking me to send him a formal letter of request giving details as to why I wanted to visit the Pakistani side of the LoC, the locations I wanted to visit, etc. I did the needful and also added, 'Who I talk to, where I go, etc. will be at the discretion of the Pakistan Army.' I had to assure Rawalpindi that mine was a purely academic visit.

Ghazi called his junior, the incumbent chief of general staff, Bilal Akbar, and requested that I be given permission to travel to the LoC. Akbar agreed to get it done, and set the ball rolling to get it vetted by other bureaucracies—most importantly, the ISI.

'What would go through your mind if you had orders to bombard central India with a Pakistani strike corps, for instance?' I once asked Ghazi. There was a reason behind this rather silly-sounding hypothetical question. He paused for a moment.

Ghazi has a deep connection with India, not only because his Pathan forefathers came to India as part of the Afghan invader Ahmed Shah Abdali's military campaign in the eighteenth century and settled here, but more importantly, both his parents migrated to Pakistan during Partition, leaving a large chunk of their family behind. Ghazi still has several close relatives living in Nagpur. During his 2006 visit to India as Defence Secretary, Ghazi requested the then Indian high commissioner in Pakistan to give him and his wife visas to travel to Nagpur to meet his relatives whom he had never met. His father, who was serving in the British Indian Army, had left for the newly created Pakistan much before Ghazi was born. He had grown up listening to stories told by his parents about India and Nagpur, about their roots, but had never had an opportunity to visit his 'ancestral land'.

The Indian side was gracious. Ghazi may not have achieved the Siachen mission given by Musharraf, but he made it to his father's home in Nagpur. Not only did the Indian government allow him to visit his family in Nagpur, but his Indian counterpart Ajai Vikram Singh arranged an Indian Air Force (IAF) aircraft to take him to Nagpur with proper escorts and protocols. 'I was received in Nagpur like a big shot by my relatives. Afshan and I were treated like newly-weds by our relatives since they had never met us. I don't think I will meet them ever again,' Ghazi had told me with a laugh tinged with nostalgia.

'I wouldn't hesitate even for a moment before leading the strike corps into the heart of India. I know it would mean death and destruction. But that's my job. My professional commitment will trump any feelings I have for my Indian friends or my own relatives in India,' Ghazi answered grimly.

The Soft-Spoken General

'How was your visit to my former office?' the soft-spoken Pakistani general asked me in Singapore at a workshop on nuclear escalation in February 2018. The no-nonsense Lieutenant General Waheed Arshad (retired) had been the director general (DG) of ISPR, and the director general planning at the chief of army staff's secretariat, both based in Rawalpindi. Put differently, he was Pakistan's military spokesperson, and prepared military plans for the Pakistan Army chief. In his mid-sixties now, Arshad is a fitness freak, and sharp when he talks, which he does with a smile. Arshad is a to-the-point man, and doesn't speak one word more than what is required. He often taunts the Indian side in track-II gatherings with backhanded remarks and smiles mischievously when he sees the other side getting rattled. In many ways, he is a complete contrast to Ghazi.

I got to know him in track-II meetings after he retired from service. I was wary of him initially—'Quite an unrelenting hardliner, this chap,' I'd think to myself. Then one evening when we sat down at the hotel lobby in Bangkok, Arshad asked me the universal question that brings people together: 'Would you like a beer?' Our friendship began with chilled Heineken Lager Beer. He spoke about his retirement life, his workout routine and family.

The 'former office' he was referring to was the office of the chief of general staff (CGS) at the Pakistan Army's General Headquarters (GHQ) in Rawalpindi, which he occupied from 2010 to 2013—one of the most powerful positions in the Pakistan Army, some say the second most powerful post after that of the chief of the army staff. Arshad, then, was the second most powerful army officer in the country for three years.

I was at his former office in Rawalpindi, inside the GHQ, three weeks before he posed that question to me.

Before retiring from service in 2013, Arshad, as the CGS, was the Pakistan Army's counterterrorism tsar. From 2010 onwards, Arshad had meticulously planned and executed Pakistan's counterterrorism operations in the Federally Administered Tribal Areas (FATA), in the badlands of north-western Pakistan. These operations were appreciated widely inside Pakistan for being highly effective in flushing out terrorists from Pakistan's tribal heartland. 'You should go to FATA and see how I cleaned it up,' he would often tell me during conversations, beaming with pride and professional satisfaction. I hope to, one day.

It was at Bangkok's Lebua Hotel that I first had a lengthy conversation with him, in April 2016. The hotel is famous for the Sky Bar which is said to be the world's highest open-air bar and is located on the sixty-fourth floor. The Sky Bar offered a bird's-eye view of everything around, a certain objectivity that was nearly always lacking when it came to the Indo-Pak conflict. My subsequent conversation with Arshad, overlooking the Bangkok cityscape and the winding Chao Phraya river, brought a lot of perspective to the components that lead to conflict, CFVs, etc.

I was keen to know his views on CFVs, given the important posts he had held in the Pakistan Army. He had been the director of military operations (DMO), the Indian equivalent of deputy director general of military operations (DGMO). He was the DMO when the 2003 November ceasefire agreement was agreed upon by India and Pakistan. His boss, Gen. Ashfaq Parvez Kayani, who later became the army chief, had made the call to the Indian DGMO Gen. A.S. Bhaiya, suggesting that the two sides stop the firing on the J&K borders. Warm and pleasant, Arshad talks with precision, clarity and sharpness—no wonder he was the Pakistan Army's chief spokesperson.

As an inquisitive researcher, I am shameless, and I ask my students to shed shame and ego at the outset of their research journey. I go up to anyone, Indian or Pakistani, who I think can give me an insight on my topic of research, and ask for a chat. And I doggedly follow up. I often get lucky.

I was inquiring into how the two armies had reached the agreement in November 2003. The several conversations that I have had with him thereafter revolved around gaining a deeper perspective on how the local military dynamics on the LoC often trigger CFVs. I was not interested in the big-picture political explanations on why fire breaks out. I wanted to know about the 'minor flares' that trigger firing between the two sides and eventually escalate.

The CFA was the result of a lot of groundwork. In the months preceding the 2003 ceasefire, the Research and Analysis Wing (RAW) chief C.D. Sahay and his ISI counterpart General Ehsan ul-Haq met in undisclosed European cities on several occasions to chalk out a ceasefire agreement. This was accepted by the two political leaderships who then asked the respective armies to implement it.

And yet, it was important for me to get more details about Gen. Kayani's call to Gen. Bhaiya. Arshad said that the CFA was to be understood in the larger context of changes in Pakistan, between India and Pakistan, and the rising violence on the J&K borders. He further told me: 'We had Kargil, then military takeover, Indian Parliament attacks, we almost went to war [. . .] There was a realization that both countries cannot afford to have this kind of situation, and it will take both countries down. You know that he [Pervez Musharraf] totally changed the Kashmir policy, and he had a lot of ground support. The military, the general public, the media, intelligence—everybody was happy that things are moving forward [. . .] so that was one of the reasons [behind] his policy provisions of improvement of relations [. . .] ceasefire was one part of the overall framework of improving of relations [. . .] you must have noticed that [. . .] the change of Kashmir policy started after that.'

'An impressive building, and an imposing office. It must have been a heady feeling, right?' I said jokingly, referring to the perks of his position as the CGS.

He laughed and said, 'Oh yes, it was!'

Arshad had played a crucial role in getting me to the Pakistani side of the LoC.

My requests, through several retired generals, to visit the Pakistani side of the LOC, were hitting a brick wall. It was simply taking too long, and no positive news was in the offing. I was almost giving up in exasperation. My Karachi visa for the first week of December didn't come through. I was told by my hosts in Karachi that the interior ministry had not cleared the visa. I was both angry and disappointed. I realized that all my efforts in the last two years were going to go down the drain. I had to do something. I texted Arshad, asking him to intervene. It's now or never, I told him.

'Give me some time,' came the reply. He promised to take my request to the GHQ personally—it was important to sort things out by personal intervention, he reasoned. He said he was visiting his former colleagues at the GHQ soon. Many of his juniors were now running the Pakistan Army, and having retired just four years ago, the general had his links at the highest levels of the army.

He called DGMO Sahir Shamshad Mirza at the Military Operations Directorate in Rawalpindi, and Bilal Akbar, the chief of general staff, before personally meeting them. When Arshad was the vice chief of general staff, Akbar had been DMO. '[Happymon Jacob] has an objective view of Indo-Pak relations; he doesn't have the conventional view on Pakistan. We should invite him to visit,' Arshad told his one-time subordinate, Bilal Akbar. The latter agreed, as did his chief, General Qamar Javed Bajwa.

Arshad also impressed the same idea upon the more sceptical individuals in Aabpara. He called up the men who were handling my case in the ISI.

Though he lives in Lahore, Arshad often travels to Rawalpindi to meet the DGMO and the CGS to brief them about the track-II work as well as to research his upcoming book on Kargil.

Arshad's personal intervention seemed to have worked. In late November I started getting somewhat positive messages including a text message from the Vasant Vihar man requesting a meeting. The 'Vasant Vihar man' later sent a positive report, highly recommending my visit. Everything was in order, and I was told it was only a matter of time before the documentation came through. But there was still no invite and visa. It was back to square one. I was giving up, in complete frustration, once again. My worst fear was that someone had torpedoed the request at the last moment. Did someone review the file and ask for a fresh look? This would invariably put an end to my carefully calibrated request for a visit to the LoC. I spent days worrying about it.

Then, all of a sudden, one evening, I heard the familiar beep of a text message. It was from Arshad: 'Happymon, your visit has got the green signal.' The message was cryptic but that was all I needed.

'What now?' I replied, impatiently.

'Call the high commission and make an appointment with the visa section,' he responded. I called the Vasant Vihar man who confirmed the news and asked me to come to the high commission for the visa.

The green signal had come from the very top. And 'the top' in Pakistan means its army. I was later told by a retired Pakistani brigadier that the visit was cleared when the chief of staff of the Pakistan Army, General Bajwa, gave it the green signal. Bajwa, so I was told, was keen that the Pakistan Army is seen as open and transparent.

Arshad, like Ghazi, also has a connection with India. His mother had migrated from Amritsar during Partition. Arshad visited India for the first time in 2004. He was Pakistan's DMO, accompanying the country's Defence Secretary to discuss Sir Creek and Siachen. Arshad recalls that New Delhi was more amenable to a mutual withdrawal proposal from Siachen during those days.

Arshad's team had proposed that the two countries mark the present positions on a map, exchange the maps and then move back to lower positions. India insisted on authentication of the line. At that point of time Pakistan had a problem with authentication since it would complicate the status of the territories that lay beyond NJ-9842.[4] By 2006, New Delhi's position would shift again, as discussed earlier.

Yet again, the Government of India had arranged an IAF aircraft to take the delegation to Agra and Fatehpur Sikri, with the 50 Parachute brigade of the Indian Army hosting them in Agra. Arshad has not visited India ever since. But he hopes to, in order to complete his book.

'What's the central thesis of the book?' I asked him when I met him in Singapore in February 2018.

'You have to wait for the book to come out. But I am making some new revelations,' he said.

'Like what?' I asked, keeping at it.

'Well, for one, I am arguing that the Kargil campaign was a well-planned one.' Arshad is right: the common-sense wisdom is that Kargil was a minor operation that went out of control. His version is bound to create uneasy chatter in the subcontinent. Arshad's thesis, in a way, disputes the logic of an operation that went out of control, as proposed by Ghazi.

I look forward to welcoming him in New Delhi, and of course, reading the book.

The Obstacle Course before the LoC

Missed Calls on the Landline

Between midnight and 1 a.m., the ivory-coloured landline in Room 310 of Lahore's Pearl Continental Hotel would ring without fail. I spent three nights there and got so used to the sound that I couldn't sleep till that blank call had cut through the sultry summer night.

It was April 2016 and I was in Pakistan with a 'Lahore-only visa' and the bottle of Glenmorangie that the Pakistani customs had failed to detect at the Wagah border. My friend and young Pakistani academic Dr Yaqoob Khan Bangash had organized a conference: 'Afkar-e-Taza: Rescuing the Past, Shaping the Future'. I was to speak at the conference. Going to Pakistan, however, was far more important to me than being at the conference.

Midnight calls and uninvited visitors belong to the dark underbelly of Indo-Pak relations, representing the worst phases. Close to one and a half years after I'd received those blank calls, the two countries continued the drill at the official level.

In March 2018, a diplomatic row broke out between New Delhi and Islamabad: the two traded allegations about the harassment of their respective diplomats by each other's intelligence agencies. India stated in its complaint that Pakistani agents would harass Indian diplomats by landing up at their Islamabad residences in the wee hours of the morning. The *Indian Express* reported on 15 March that the doorbell of the Indian deputy high commissioner in Islamabad, J.P. Singh, had been rung at 3 a.m.

Negativity almost never goes unanswered. A few days later, Pakistan's deputy high commissioner's residence in New Delhi had a visitor around the same time. As the diplomatic row escalated, Pakistan recalled its high commissioner for consultations. It had become a complete diplomatic game of tit-for-tat, with diplomats' cars getting waylaid, and agents on bikes harassing diplomats and their families in full public view. Young children watched from inside the cars how grown-up nations behave just as they do at lunch break.

Actually, they have been at it for a long time. My friends in the diplomatic community say that it used to be worse. In the early 1990s, during the initial years of the insurgency in Kashmir and the heightened fears of an India–Pakistan military escalation, it had become particularly difficult for diplomats to work in each other's countries. So the two foreign secretaries reached an agreement on the treatment of diplomatic personnel. They agreed to a code of conduct in August 1992 that year 'to protect diplomatic personnel, guaranteeing them freedom from harassment'. What is even more interesting was that the two sides further decided to translate the code of conduct into Hindi and Urdu and make it available to local police stations near the diplomatic areas and lower-ranking police officials. After all, the ones who knocked on doors at 3 a.m. were unlikely to have heard of the 1961 Vienna Convention, which deals with the treatment of diplomatic personnel.

I was irritated at first, but the late-night phone calls in Lahore eventually aroused my curiosity. I was spooked and yet the city maintained its attraction for me. Lahore, for a great many Indians, is an 'enemy' city. In the event of a full-scale conventional war between India and Pakistan, the city is sure to be bombed out. Lahore most likely occupies a special place in the 'target list' of the Indian war planners. The Amritsar Cantonment of the Indian Army is around 50 kilometres away, its strike corps based in Ambala is around 270 kilometres away, and strike aircraft from India's Adampur Air Force Base would take barely a few minutes to rain bombs over Lahore. The spiritedly hospitable Lahorites wouldn't know what hit them. If nuclear weapons are used, things would get far worse. In a course that I taught at JNU, on nuclear strategy, we often discussed the yields required to send Lahore back to the Stone Age, even as we realized that nuking Lahore would have a serious blowback effect on India.

In an enemy city, the unfailing nightly call made me feel as though someone was looking after me, checking up to see if all was well. I was on someone's mindscape. I felt cared for, even if it was an invasive manner of caring. This was the kind of attention you didn't know what to do with.

The hotel, popularly referred to as PC by Lahorites, was established by Sadruddin Hashwani in 1960, in the famous Gulberg area. The hotel is not too far from the Liberty Market and the Governor's House. PC is easily one of the best hotels in Lahore. The walk from the lobby to the car park is long and slow. There's a standard security check at the main gate and two more along the 500-metre walk, until you finally get to the person smiling at you behind the wooden circular desk. The walk is well worth it, though—the Nadia Coffee Shop on the ground floor of the hotel offers mouth-watering Lahori delicacies, from halwa-puri to hareesa.

By the third day, I had gotten used to the midnight drill. I'd pick up the receiver after a couple of rings, only to hear radio silence and then the nearly extinct old-world 'click' of someone hanging up.

I considered having a little fun and putting the receiver off the handle—a little personal justice for keeping me up every night, but I didn't want any visitors landing up at 3 a.m. Moreover, I was being tailed on a daily basis from the moment I left the hotel. Why call for unnecessary trouble?

I was followed religiously through the day, from the breakfast table till I retired to my room. There was never a lonely moment, not when you had company in such close proximity. At breakfast, the minders, as they are called, would sit on the chairs in the lobby outside the coffee shop facing the restaurant, keeping me under observation. They would hurriedly follow me on their motorbikes as soon as I boarded a vehicle to go out into the city and later ask me the details of whoever I met. I made it a point to discourage most of my Lahori friends from coming over to meet me.

Lahore, to me, signifies everything I love about Pakistan. This cultural capital of Pakistan has excellent food streets, history, culture, evening qawwali performances, loud music, dusty busy alleys and warm hospitable Lahorites. Lahore is a bit worn down with history, having been home to a multitude of civilizations. Burka-clad women, young girls wearing jeans and lipstick, men in Pathan suits and schoolkids chatting away: sometimes you mistake it for the by-lanes of old Delhi. There's life in Lahore, and it's welcoming and happening. Were there Indian spies lurking around the city's dusty by-lanes, on a recce to spot potential recruits? I often wondered. Or perhaps they mostly operated in Islamabad and New Delhi. I had heard many stories about Lahore's drug runners and their well-oiled links across the border in the Indian Punjab.

I am almost always in a dilemma when in Lahore. How do I intellectualize this city of 11 million people? As a red mark on my country's nuclear-targeting list? As the cultural capital of a 'terrorist nation'? As the missing piece to what should have been independent India? Home to some of my dear friends, their families and kids? Or the base of Pakistan's IV Corps which is likely to wreak havoc in India should there be another military confrontation between India and Pakistan? I have a deep love for the city, a city that has 'treacherously' allowed the passage of invading armies—from the Aryans to the Mongols—across its borders and into the Indian heartland. Not that I love old Delhi any less than Lahore's walled city, but the enchantment of the enemy is not amenable to reason or patriotism. Isn't jealousy deeply embedded in our notions of enmity and hatred, and nationalism? Nationalism sanctions and promotes jealousy in a systematic manner. Aren't there times when we hate the 'Other' more than we love ourselves? Are there times when the only rationale for the 'Us' is the 'Other'?

This is not just about Lahore. It's about Pakistan and Pakistanis in general—the mortal fascination of the enemy that I am unable to shake off. Is being fascinated by your enemy treacherous, or is it self-love in reverse?

A mention of India (they prefer 'Hindustan', a term I intensely dislike; 'It's India,' I kept correcting them in vain) in Lahore would meet with welcome smiles, quick conversations and a likely discount especially in those hole-in-the-wall shops. Even invitations home from complete strangers. Upscale shops have no sense of nostalgia, I figured; it's the old bearded men selling rusty wares who have a sense of nostalgic history—the same type you normally associate with extreme views about India. And the people of Lahore may even have seen the latest Bollywood flick that you haven't. They love

India—well, most of them do. The ones who say they don't are jealous, I would imagine. I am exaggerating my point here, but to stress the warm feelings common Pakistanis have towards India.

I don't care too much about haters on either side of the dividing line. I often half-jokingly tell my friends that the India–Pakistan problem is something that north Indians and Pakistani Punjabis have to settle among themselves. The misconceptions we have about Pakistanis, and vice versa, are rooted in unfamiliarity. Let people travel back and forth and you will see the difference. Beyond that, political agendas have tended a tree of hate that continues to blossom and feeds our impressions of those on the other side.

But isn't there still a political, if not moral, dilemma about being neutral about Pakistan, South Asia's insatiable revisionist, home of the 'ever-scheming' Pakistani fauj? Am I being naive, as many of my retired diplomat friends insist? Or have I been entrapped by the unending postmodern desires of my curious academic quests?

The minders would 'see me off' near the lift in the middle of the lobby at the hotel. I think they secretly hoped that I wouldn't venture out after that. They would never say so, but it was evident on their tired faces—riding a worn-out motorbike through the city chasing a car on a hot summer day is not so easy. More so, they had their homes to get back to.

The midnight phone call was to make sure that I hadn't left the room after they saw me off, I later gathered. Not that they would stop me from going out—they would just give me company. In a sense, I was being charitable towards them by not going out late night. It was as though I had developed a certain friendliness towards them, on the sly. These were people doing a job which was part of a policy that they had no hand in making.

I wanted to visit Lahore's famous Data Darbar to watch a qawwali performance, which is regularly organized at the tomb of Data Ganj Bakhsh, the eleventh-century Muslim saint. It would have to be a late-evening outing. But I decided against the trip—what if I missed the missed call on my landline?

On day three, after the conference, I waited for the call. I was kind of excited about the whole experience: the enviable thrill of being the accidental protagonist of a self-imagined fast-paced spy movie. It was far more attention than I deserved, and had hoped for. As midnight arrived, I impatiently looked at the phone. I knew it would ring any time: they had to make sure that I was in the room.

I was with a new-found friend from London, whom I had met during the conference; we were chatting late into the night. I had insisted on being in my room, for obvious reasons. As we talked, I occasionally glanced at the phone.

At around 12.30 a.m., the phone rang, as expected. I rushed to the landline and picked up the receiver.

'Hello,' I paused for a second and said in Hindi/Urdu, 'I am in my room.' I replaced the receiver on the holder soon after.

My friend was surprised—'What was that about?' I smiled reassuringly.

'That was the goodnight call from my minders,' I told my friend, who continued to look deeply puzzled, and a wee bit worried. The friend, though ethnically Indian, had a British passport and hence had no minders.

The friend left soon thereafter, seemingly a bit nervous.

'You Are on a No-Entry List'

A heady mix of curiosity and fear had me contemplating one question throughout my four-day journey with the Pakistani army. What did a 'no-entry list' mean and why was I on it?

It was in his aesthetically done-up basement drawing room that the Vasant Vihar man had told me, days before I visited PoK, 'You are on a no-entry list. That's why your Karachi visa never came through. I am doing everything I can to get you off that list.' I was dying of curiosity and an inexplicable sense of tension. What could be the reason for it? At what level had the decision been taken? Who had taken it?

But I hadn't pestered him—I'd had bigger fish to fry. Visiting PoK was far more crucial than getting answers to my anxious questions. I let the tension inside me build up, like a plot.

It was only upon my return to Delhi that I decided to bring up the subject with the Vasant Vihar man again. I had to get an answer, now that I had returned; intellectual curiosities also need closure. And this one wasn't purely intellectual.

We met for lunch and the Vasant Vihar man picked out a table at the far end of the restaurant. He sat with his back to the wall in order to get an overview of everyone present there. If a patron or a waiter passed our table, he would stop talking and resume the conversation once they were out of earshot. These were the kind of measures you would expect in a spy movie and I wasn't surprised. This must have been part of his training for the current position he held.

There was a Cold War Eastern European feel to our meeting. While on sabbatical in Budapest I once went on a Cold War tour of the city called 'Spies and Masters: Cold War Tour of Budapest'. Scenes from the Budapest tour guide's colourful and embellished descriptions of spy confabulations in cafes in the city's Jewish quarter suddenly flashed in my mind. The Vasant Vihar man would often scan the restaurant for anything unusual and wait for the waiter to leave before he resumed the conversation. Not that I was telling him anything secret—nor did I have any secrets to tell, but I guess he had to be careful.

'There is a reason why I selected this place for a chat.' He paused, and looked around, carefully and cautiously. 'My minders would find it tough to pay for a meal here and more so find it even more difficult to snoop on my conversation.'

The Vasant Vihar man had his minders in India, just as I had mine while in Pakistan. While most Indians visiting Pakistan talk of spooks tailing them, not all Pakistani friends visiting India talk of similar experiences. More interestingly, minders in Pakistan will be hardly dissuaded by upscale restaurants or posh hotels. They would, for instance, sit right outside the Zamana restaurant on the ground floor of the Serena Hotel in Islamabad, carefully observing who you were talking to, and scribbling in pocket-sized notebooks, as if they could read your lips. Or it was just to let you know you were being watched, from such close quarters—sort of deterrence. They wouldn't hesitate for a minute to walk into the restaurant and perch themselves on a chair right behind you, and the hotel staff would merely look on, helplessly. That would be impossible in India. New Delhi, in that sense, is not all that spook-friendly.

I had my guesses about why I was on a no-entry list. I asked my friends and track-II colleagues in Pakistan—they were as puzzled as I was. I sought an appointment with the Vasant Vihar man as soon as I returned home and he gladly obliged. He also wanted to ask me how India looked from the other side: 'Were you able to see it from our perspective?'

'Well, in a geographical sense, yes,' and I laughed; he joined in.

'Now tell me, why did you guys put me on a no-entry list?' I asked him. He looked up from the restaurant's elaborate menu, glanced at me and then at the waiter—he wanted to wait till we were alone.

'Someone may have read something you wrote and decided that your writings do not show Pakistan in good light. He may have written something in some file . . . You see, once it is in the file, it's difficult to change it. It's sorted out now.'

Despite his vagueness, here was the answer I was looking for all this while. But that made me even more anxious. His simple, straightforward answer raised several more questions: So they have a file on me? What kind of file? What do they have in it? Is it regularly updated? I felt both important and worried at the same time—the Pakistani agencies had a file on me!

Not that he sounded unconvincing, but for some reason I had this strange feeling that it was more than just what I had written that may have landed me in trouble. There was a specific reason why I thought so.

Minders on a Motorbike

I hadn't noticed them until I arrived at the reception of the Pearl Continental on a humid day in June 2016. I had taken a cab from the Wagah border to the hotel; it was unlikely they had followed me from the border. But they sure knew I would check into this exact hotel and the approximate time. That's smart intelligence work.

Their clothing made them stand out from the other hotel guests and I realized they *wanted* to be noticed. They made no secret of their mission, asking the receptionist for a copy of my passport and tickets right in front of me. Their in-your-face attitude sent a straightforward signal: 'You're being watched, behave yourself.'

The young receptionist who stood diagonally opposite to me in the circular reception area hardly looked surprised, nor did she resist. But she did throw a glance at me—more to express her helplessness than to seek permission. I shrugged nonchalantly. I was taking it in my stride. This was, after all, not my first visit to Pakistan. I wasn't going to get caught up in needless fights. The whole affair looked pretty normal and regular. Everyone seemed to know their part of the drill: the guard at the gate never stopped the motorcycle, the receptionist didn't hesitate, the men didn't bother, and I knew it was coming. It was a well-rehearsed charade.

'What was that about?' I asked the receptionist later when I came down to the reception. She looked embarrassed and hadn't thought I would ask that question out of the blue. I smiled reassuringly to put her at ease, and to indicate that I wasn't going to make a scene. 'Am I in some kind of trouble?' I was trying to get into her mind.

'No, no, not at all . . . It's a routine security check for foreign nationals.' I asked her if it was routine for them to give copies of the documents of all foreigners visiting the hotel or whether it was only those of Indians. This time she evaded my question: 'I am not sure, sir, I am new here. You'd have to talk to my manager.' She pointed towards an older man. I didn't bother to go up to him.

A retired Pakistani general, who had had a stint in the ISI, once gave me a general piece of advice on how to deal with minders: 'Be nice to them and chat them up.' Their brief is a straightforward one—follow you like a shadow and report back. They had the authority to ask you questions that you didn't have to answer. However, being cocky with them would just result in unnecessary harassment. These men were simply doing their job, one that senior officials considered tedious and lowly. The best way to deal with your tail is to humanize them and understand their predicament. Granted, it's irritating being followed around but it's got to be worse for those doing the following.

In short, they had no brief to trouble you unless you pissed them off. So, I wasn't going to piss them off at any cost.

The lanky younger minder had the look of a rookie who was eager and persistent. He was constantly vigilant and a direct contrast to his partner. The stockier, shorter one was more relaxed and looked half bored. He knew the drill, and usually let his novice take the lead while following me on foot. Otherwise, the 'boys' stalked me on a run-down motorcycle. All they had to do was whisper into the guard's ear and he would let them into the hotel compound without a security check.

One night they barged into my room.

'Someone from security wants to meet you,' the receptionist had told me shortly before the event. I promised to be down soon but the 'boys' couldn't wait. The fact that I had a friend in my room must have been a cause for concern. The doorbell rang in less than a minute or so. They must have run up the stairs to reach the third floor in such a short time.

They ignored my greeting and walked right in. The younger one sat on the edge of my bed. 'What brings you here?' he asked. They were shabbily dressed but they made up for it with an abundance of confidence.

'A conference,' I replied.

'What are you speaking on? Who will you meet here?'

The questions came quick and fast. They knew the answers but they were simply cross-checking to see if I'd slip up.

They eyed the Glenmorangie bottle and my friend as if to say, 'how can a Muslim drink?' Or they may have simply taken a fancy to the golden Scotch sparkling in the tall, elegant bottle. Either way, it was unnerving.

My friend, a former Pakistani civil servant, suggested this was no way to treat a guest from across the border. They ignored him. 'We're simply doing our job,' said the older minder. My friend knew how these agencies functioned and he went on. 'I have served in the government,' he said. 'This is not how things work and you're crossing your limits.'

'Times are different now,' said the rookie, and put an end to my friend's objections.

The younger minder kept up the barrage of questions for another ten minutes while the older one surveyed the room. 'Are you going out later tonight?' asked the rookie.

'Not today,' I replied.

That was it. They left the way they came in, skipping niceties. I realized I had been wrong about the younger minder. He was no greenhorn going by the way he took control of the questioning while sitting on my hotel bed.

The elderly gentleman who was visiting me in the room told me to take it easy. 'Of course, I know the drill,' I responded reassuringly.

Despite my experience with minders I was slightly thrown off by their behaviour. Why all this haste and crudeness? Did something happen? I later found out that the Kulbhushan Jadhav case had something to do with the increased surveillance.

I had to hand it to them. Sitting at a desk and tailing a person were jobs that were poles apart. The latter was about zero subtlety. And yet, the minders had found a way to find out what I was up to without being overly aggressive. I respected them for that.

Resistance wouldn't help. My next strategy was name-dropping, and I know quite a few high-profile names in Pakistan, the kind of names that mattered. Dropping names of Pakistani politicians wouldn't help. Knowing a couple of current generals would make it easier but I didn't know any personally. So I went with the retired generals—I knew several of them. I talked about them, their careers, how I knew them and how I would be dining with them while in Lahore (all of which was accurate).

Junior officers like to listen to gossip about their seniors. In Pakistan, where the army has a larger-than-life image and place in the society, talking about your proximity to senior army officers, albeit retired ones, can get you a lot of attention.

The minders started getting friendly. The older chap continued to be bored and uninterested, but I had managed to provoke the curiosity of the lanky guy.

They started to smile and talk about inconsequential things. The change in their behaviour was unmissable. I thought I had got them where I wanted them. But I was to be proven wrong soon.

Minders are usually low-ranking officers who don't bother with sophisticated behaviour—a crucial reason why I didn't want to cross them.

The boys followed me everywhere on their gas-guzzling motorcycle. I also made it a point to inform them of my plans while in Lahore. The quid pro quo was clear: I would be nice to them, and they would make my life less difficult.

'He is our guest, don't overcharge him.' The young minder instructed the autorickshaw driver who was taking me to Anarkali Bazaar. I was pleasantly surprised when they helped me choose the best local items to take back to India. They haggled with the Anarkali shopkeepers, suggested places to visit and curios to buy. They glanced at their wristwatches impatiently as I rummaged through the second-hand bookstalls in the back alleys of Anarkali Bazaar. They still made notes, never let me out of their sight and constantly consulted each other in whispers. However, the surveillance was slowly beginning to feel like guardianship, with a pinch of camaraderie thrown in for good measure. Nonetheless, they kept at their primary job—ensuring I didn't do anything without them knowing about it.

The shopkeepers not only gave me good discounts but treated me with respect. Why wouldn't they? Here I was, going about with two men whose demeanour suggested they were from the security services.

I felt special—that rousing feeling of self-importance in an alien land. Despite the hassle that came with it, I started looking forward to being tailed—it was so much fun. I was disappointed when I wasn't followed in December 2018. 'Why wasn't I followed during my 2018 visit?' I asked a friend who knew the system.

'Who would tail you when you are the guest of the Pakistan Army?' he responded.

But there was more to the story on why the tailing was so thorough this time in Lahore—namely Kulbhushan Jadhav, whom Pakistan alleged was an Indian spy, something the Indian authorities denied, claiming he had been kidnapped by Pakistan. The Pakistanis alleged that he was being handled by RAW under orders from the Indian NSA, Ajit Doval. Pakistan accused Jadhav of carrying out terror activities in Baluchistan. To add to their claim, they kept repeating what NSA Doval had said in a speech in 2014 before he had become Modi's NSA: 'You can do one Mumbai, you may lose Balochistan.'[1] It's a different matter that Doval had made the statement before he was appointed the NSA.

It turned out that all Indians in Pakistan were put under intrusive surveillance at the time. New visas were not being approved easily, and even the people who were granted one were restricted to a city or two at best. I had asked for a three-city visa but was granted a 'Lahore only' visa.

'All Indians are under the scanner,' I was told by a retired Pakistani official when I complained of unprecedented surveillance.

This wasn't the first time. Every time I was in Pakistan, I was tailed, without exception. The first time was in March 2006 when I was staying at the Serena Hotel in Islamabad.

I was there for a Pugwash conference. There were 'men from the security services' roaming the corridors outside our hotel rooms, and seated across the Zamana restaurant on the ground floor. But they would keep a distance and ensured discretion. There would be no eye contact, period. Try engaging them, they would walk away. The tradition of distance and discretion continued, until 2016.

Intruder at the Lahore Cantonment

The boys on the old, run-down motorbike suddenly sped past our SUV, blocked the busy highway and vigorously signalled the driver to stop. The man riding the bike didn't seem to bother with the SUV driver's angry reactions right outside the main entrance of the Lahore Cantonment.

Annoyed and puzzled, the driver of the imposing black SUV had no choice but to stop—the motorbike was right in the middle of the road. The other occupants of the SUV, besides myself, were its driver and what appeared to be the security detail of a retired four-star general of the Pakistan Army. The general, who had retired not too long ago, had sent me his private vehicle with his driver and the bodyguard. The latter seemed to be a serving army soldier. The boys didn't know whose car it was, nor did the men in the car know who the boys on the bike were. I knew them both.

I was to be at dinner with the general and a retired CGS, in the former's house inside the Lahore Cantonment. The boys sure weren't aware of whose guest they were waylaying. A former chairman of the Joint Chiefs of Staff Committee, who happens to be a retired army general, and a recently retired CGS of the Pakistan Army were two unquestionably powerful people in Pakistan, while in office. And in the Pakistani scheme of things, a four-star general and a two-star general retain a great deal of power, despite retirement. The men who took direct orders from these two generals were running the Pakistan Army—some would say, the country.

The driver and the bodyguard alighted from the car to ask why the car was being blocked. There was no way I could listen to what exactly they were arguing about from inside the car, though I could see the tableau of angry questions, firm responses and quick phone calls. I could guess what was going on: the SUV was carrying an Indian citizen—whose visa to Pakistan stated 'not valid for restricted/prohibited area'—and was about to enter the Lahore Cantonment. I was about to violate my visa rules. Or had I violated them already? I felt safe inside the well-guarded SUV but that sense of safety could well have been illusory.

The minders knew I was going to someone's home for dinner (I had told them as much), but they didn't know who it was, and it had skipped my mind to give them the details regarding my hosts. They had followed me routinely. It was only at the entrance of the cantonment when they realized that the evening was going to be more than routine.

The military police manning the gate came rushing to the scene. The muscular soldiers in army fatigues with AK-47s slung across their chests arrived accompanied by the unarmed military policemen. They recognized the driver and the bodyguard and greeted them in a friendly manner. The soldiers asked the boys to remove their bike and let the car pass, but the boys held their ground and said they wouldn't let the car pass with me in it. Was it simply their stubbornness or blind confidence in whoever had ordered them to tail me? I couldn't differentiate from inside the car. But the boys seemed to have prevailed over the soldiers.

The driver walked back to the SUV and filled me in. He said they had informed the general and that I would eventually be allowed to go inside. It was only a matter of time, they assured me. Despite such assurances, situations like this are hard not to worry about, especially when you're on the other side of the border. I was in clear visa violation, 'caught' at the gate of a military cantonment trying to enter without proper authorization—all this taking place at a time when the Pakistani security establishment was jacking up the surveillance on Indians in Pakistan, thanks to the Kulbhushan incident. Depending on how a Pakistani official looked at it, it could be a minor visa violation or a security threat. What if the Pakistani media got wind of it? How would they frame the whole affair? What if one of those overzealous Indian channels got to know of it? How would they treat the news? 'What was a JNU professor doing in a Pakistani cantonment?' My presence there had a lot more political implications than I had imagined sitting inside that car.

Despite these uneasy thoughts I was unusually calm. I was kind of enjoying the drama unfolding on a busy Pakistani highway. I wish I could have gotten closer to their conversation but I had been given strict orders—'Please don't come out of the car.' I wanted closer proximity to the action—perhaps to startle them with a little enemy presence and a selfie with the Lahore Cantonment in the backdrop. How about a selfie with the mayhem in the backdrop?!

The minders were quick to act and called their boss, who arrived at the scene almost immediately. The short, bald man in a short-sleeved untucked shirt whipped out his notebook and scribbled down what every party had to say: his boys, the general's man, and the military police manning the gate. What's with all this note-taking, I thought. Instead of resolving the issue, he rung up someone else. By then, the general had sent another two men to sort out the confusion. A few more armed men and military police appeared on the scene. Now the public were interested in what was going on and the military police had to constantly ask them to keep moving.

I got some curious looks from the slow-moving vehicles—but thankfully none of them thought of making a short video with me in the frame! The military personnel peeked into the car from time to time to look at the person keeping them busy as the Monday evening traffic was disrupted.

The general's men kept returning to the car, to reassure the general sahib's guest from India that he needn't worry and that it would all be sorted out. I offered to return to PC. I didn't want any trouble for myself, I told them. They wouldn't entertain my suggestion.

There was some quick chatter on the mobiles and walkie-talkies. The driver was asked to move the car to what looked like a service lane. Suddenly there was a silence. There was a palpable build-up of tension, everyone looked anxious and restless, and some quick, quiet consultations went on. Onlookers were dismissed and the whole area was cleared except for passing vehicles. It was as if they were waiting for something important to happen. And it did.

Within a few minutes, another SUV arrived on the scene. The senior officer, the bald man in the half-sleeve shirt, went up to the car and stood in attention. The window glass was rolled down, but no one stepped out. The officer kept talking to those seated inside the car while not changing his posture. He looked tense and worried. The military police stood stiffly behind the officer after saluting those inside the car. The boys looked sheepish. They neither spoke, nor were spoken to. All their bravado and self-importance seemed to disappear quickly. They looked as if they knew they were in trouble, but they also seemed to know that they had to do what they did. Theirs was an understandable dilemma.

The conversation didn't go on for too long—everything was over in three minutes, from the time the car arrived till it left. No vehicles were stopped thereafter by thereafter, nor did anyone say anything to anyone. There was decorum and discipline, and tension and fear. Someone came up to our car and asked the driver to follow the new car. 'You have temporary permission to go inside the cantonment,' the general's bodyguard stepped into the car and announced, still in a hushed tone as if those in the other car could hear him. He sounded relieved, and his smile seemed a wee bit triumphant.

'I hope this won't go into my file and be used to deny me a visa the next time I apply?' I asked the general's man when driving to the general's home.

'Of course not,' he said.

We followed the car and entered the Lahore Cantonment. Wide, well-lit streets, houses with lawns and the occasional soldier in uniform—the whole place looked prim and proper. The cars finally stopped in front of a house. The two generals alighted from the second SUV.

'Welcome to my home, professor. Hope you didn't have to sit in the car for too long.' The general smiled as we walked into the house. The boys and their motorbike waited outside, behind the cars—they just wouldn't let go.

Cut to December 2017 and I was confident of being issued a Pakistani visa for a conference in Karachi organized by a former cabinet secretary of Pakistan. I was denied a visa, without being given a reason.

Was it because of something I wrote? Or was it because of that fateful dinner inside the Lahore Cantonment? I still have no idea, but to this day a visa into Pakistan continues to be a problem. In April 2018, I applied again, to attend a Lahore University conference. My host from Lahore rang me up to say that Pakistan's interior ministry had not even bothered processing the visa application form. You never know what works in your favour and what doesn't.

Guest of the Enemy Forces

'It Will Be a Pity If You Were to Be Shot by Your Country's Army'

'That's your notorious jungle post.' Brigadier Noor was pointing at an Indian Army post perched on the upper reaches of the Pir Panjal mountain range, not too far from the Indian town of Poonch in J&K. I peeped out the window of the army jeep in the foothills of the mountain range. 'Notorious' because according to him, the men in the post, hidden away behind the dense foliage, fired at Pakistani soldiers and villages at will, causing death and destruction.

'Why would they do that?' I retorted.

'*Marzi hai* [because they feel like it],' Noor responded, adding, 'It's a free-for-all on your side, no one cares.'

Noor was not wrong. On the LoC, troops often fire for the heck of it. On the IB outside J&K, they never fire except during wars. What he didn't say, however, was that both sides do so. The 'at will' firing has diverse origins: pure boredom and factors arising out of a military culture of establishing one's moral ascendency, among others.[1]

Sometimes the reasons may be purely 'personal'. Retired Pakistani general Sikander Afzal once told me that 'monotony-breaking will also include shooting holes in clothes left for drying by the troops on the other side of the border. There are few avenues for entertainment.' And sometimes the soldiers fire for pure fun, with no intention to harm the other side. Referring to the 1980s, senior Pakistani general Ghazi told me how CFVs were often a result of gamesmanship and mirth, caused by '[. . .] silly occasions such as when you have visitors, for instance, senior officials, college students or even families [. . .] You want to show them this live fire and drama being staged and so you initiate a CFV. That was gamesmanship. Both sides engaged in it, and when one side was doing it the other would just tuck themselves in and wait for it to get over.'

Then there is the more serious firing, to establish one's moral ascendency. Former corps commander in Srinagar General Hasnain says that 'on the LoC, there is a concept called moral ascendancy—"I am the better army" and "I dominate you by my morale, training, capability". It is a macho game that adversaries in eyeball-to-eyeball contact indulge in.' Retired Indian brigadier Arun Sahgal added to the story: 'Through your domination and positions in that area, and constantly keeping the other's head down by continuous fire, you are assuring your moral ascendancy.'

If I were in an academic gathering back in JNU, I would have attempted to explain 'at will' firing using the concept of 'autonomous military factors' and pointed out that this was normal on both sides. Except that I was now on the LoC myself, with the enemy army. I steered clear of academic jargon. I didn't even tell Noor that both sides would engage in such 'at will' firing. I didn't have to; he knew it.

However, Noor's phrase—'your notorious jungle post'— did invoke an assortment of emotions in me, temporarily 'testing my sense of loyalty' to India as I couldn't help harbouring an instinctive feeling of attachment, friendliness and no ill will towards the Pakistani side. Here I was, travelling with the enemy forces. I did break bread with them, slept in their guest room, travelled in their jeeps. Their armed soldiers surrounded me, night and day, ensuring that no harm came to me from anywhere, including the 'enemy forces', i.e., the Indian troops.

But I am an Indian and, more so, was similarly treated on the other side of the line. So was it all right for me to have been momentarily loyal to my temporary hosts? Should I or should I not wish that my former hosts are among those killed when I hear of the next CFV in the Battal sector? Should I be relieved if the reports were to say that 'there were no military casualties'? What did it mean when I wished the Pakistani officers 'good luck with your work', given that their work involved firing at the Indian soldiers, which often meant killing them? Did it mean that I wished them success in their mission?

In short, whose side should I choose, psychologically and morally speaking? The Indian men manning the jungle post who might fire at the jeep in which I was travelling or the Pakistani men who were ensuring that I didn't get shot by the Indians in the jungle post? The position I was in came with several predicaments: of being an Indian, of being cared for by the Pakistani forces, of realizing the elemental absurdity of the situation.

It might appear to be simple and straightforward, but in reality, it was not: at one level, there was a major existential dilemma which confused my sense of nationalism and patriotism a great deal. But even more so, it was like having a transcendental view of the mundane while at the same time having to live with it.

Patriotism is a virtue because it makes life simple. It spares you the moral dilemmas since you don't have to feel bad when the enemy soldier or civilian—someone's father, mother or even a young kid—gets killed by a bullet or maimed by an anti-personnel landmine. Patriotism can help you ignore it, justify it, even demand such deaths—it's not a kid who got maimed for life, but a Pakistani, or for the other side, an Indian. Patriotism helps you aim at the heart of another human being through the lens of your sniper rifle across the zero line, and shoot to kill him, and then feel proud of it, and be promoted. The 'Other' can bring out the worst in us. Wars allow human collectivities to let off steam by way of organized killing.

'Are you ready for a once-in-a-lifetime adventure? Are you the adventurous type?' said Noor. A moment ago, he had asked his driver and gunman to sit at the back and gestured me to sit next to him after occupying the driver's seat himself. Would I have been where I was on that day if I were not adventurous? I was being driven along the Pakistani side of the LoC by the brigade commander, whose men manned the line, fired at the Indians and took cover when the Indians returned fire. The Indian posts were a little more than a kilometre away, from where the Indian Army soldiers would observe enemy movement through the peepholes. Perhaps they were looking for a good target and an appropriate time to fire.

Noor knows his trade. A tall, lean man with sharp features, he speaks little and when he does his words make an impact. That's the kind of men you will find commanding the forward brigades and units on the LoC on either side: the no-nonsense type, the type who would not think twice when orders came down to shoot, to kill or to be killed. The battle-hardened, follow-the-orders-without-questions type.

I had no reason to say no—this drive was exactly what I had been looking for all along. I had arrived at Rawalakot from Muzaffarabad the previous evening, and had been driven for another two hours or so early in the morning to get to the LoC, for a 'piece of the action'—and 'a piece of the action', well almost, was exactly what Noor was offering, as if he had read my mind.

But there was a reason why Noor was asking if I was the adventurous type: this particular area to which we were travelling had been a regular target of the Indian forces, given their geographically superior position. Or in army lingo, Indians were 'dominating that stretch'. Firing would begin for no reason and would wreak havoc in the nearby villages. Pakistani forces tried not to provoke the Indian side, again due to locational disadvantage.

We had just finished a long meeting with the CFV victims in the Dharmsal village and were on our way to the Tatrinote–Chakan Da Bagh trading point. The region falls under the Battal sector (which the Pakistan Army calls a 'hot' area due to the frequent firing taking place there). It is on the front lines of the Rawalakot-based 2-AK brigade (what the Indian side refers to as the 2-PoK brigade), under the Murree division commanded by Major General Azhar Abbas, whom I had met the day before. For the Pakistani side it was one of the most dangerous spots: an area where Indians exercised domination through observation and firing, and the Pakistani side had to be careful due to the presence of the Pakistani civilian population living bang on the LoC. Why didn't they take me to a place where the Pakistan Army was dominating? I imagined they wanted to showcase the 'Indian atrocities' to a visiting Indian.

On the LoC, an officer's rank determines his sense of fear, hope and pain. For junior officers, in situations such as this, the morale will be down, egos will be hurt, and there is every chance they will have to witness heart-rending civilian casualties and injuries, often with no end in sight. For Noor, a brigadier, the situation was different. There were several other places where he could put the Indian side under pressure. In other words, while a lower-ranking officer has a limited area to take care of, all of which could sometimes be a location of disadvantage, the brigadier would have a larger area with physical features that dominated the other side as well as those dominated by the other side. This enables him to extract revenge, a luxury unavailable to a junior officer.

Noor insisted on taking a circuitous route, across inhospitable terrain. The jeep made its way over a pebbled road, raising dust and dry leaves, manoeuvring past cattle and potholes. Curious kids who were playing in the mud waved at us, the occasional brave one saluting the men in uniform. The faster road to the trading point was right below the Indian posts and was under constant Indian firing.

'It will be a pity if you were to be shot by your country's army,' Noor said half-seriously, explaining why he was taking the longer route instead of the much better paved and shorter route. I turned to Noor in the driver's seat to gauge the seriousness of his statement and thought to myself that ducking 'friendly fire' while on 'enemy territory' was a sensible suggestion. I promptly agreed, not that I had much of a choice. Besides the famed 'jungle post' there were several Indian posts, including K.G. Top, that could target our vehicle.

Frankly, I took his words lightly at first, but he seemed serious and recollected how a patrol party was fired at a few days ago and how the village in front of us has been under constant fire. 'Let's hope there will be no firing today.' His words weren't fully reassuring. 'This is what life on the line looks like. I thought it was important you got a taste of the tension around here.'

'What if they [the Indians] fire?' I was worried. He said his men were alert in the Pakistani posts, which would be noticed by the Indians, and there was therefore a likelihood of calm. It sounded like he was taking a huge chance.

'But if they fire, we will retaliate'—nor did that promise help.

Life on the line can be scary. I remember a retired inspector general (IG) of the BSF once telling me about the fear of sniper fire and how sniping takes a serious toll on the morale of the forces: 'A man standing on duty at the post is always under tremendous fear of being watched by the opposite side through a telescopic rifle and of being shot at any moment.'

'You could get sniped at through the peephole of the bunker if the enemy is determined, and it has happened in the past,' an Indian Army soldier in Kashmir told me, responding to my observation that well-fortified bunkers would be a safe place to be in during times of tension.

In short, you could get shot at if you are in a moving vehicle, standing guard in an exposed post or sitting in your fortified bunker having a quick lunch. That must be a scary existence. I was getting a ringside view of a soldier's daily life. For me it was like 'fear tourism': imagine the fear that you could be killed any time and having to get used to that.

My uneasy smile veiled a tense self and several worldly worries: What if something happens to me here? What if I get shot or hit by a mortar splinter? Would they take me to the Combined Military Hospital in Rawalakot? Does my Bajaj Allianz travel insurance cover bullet injuries in Pakistan? Perhaps not. How will I travel back to Delhi with a bullet/ splinter injury? What will I tell those who ask who shot me? That I was shot by the Indian Army? What will the Indian authorities tell my family back in Delhi as to what happened to me—'He was shot by us while on the Pakistani side'? How will my toddler explain it when he grows up—'Baba was shot by Indian soldiers while in Pakistan'?

But those troubling and, perhaps silly, worries in the gut were outweighed by sheer excitement, by a sense of professional achievement of having done something no Indian academic has probably ever done before me—driving around in a Pakistani army jeep on the LoC, ducking Indian bullets.

Before we started our journey, Noor had left his commander's vehicle behind a bridgehead under the cover of trees. He had travelled to Battal village below the Indian posts in an unmarked jeep without the brigadier insignia. I noticed it right away. 'Why has he left his official vehicle behind? Does he think he would be targeted?' I asked my liaison officer. He just smiled and said nothing.

Perhaps Noor didn't want the Indian Army to identify him and take shots at a high-value target. Not that soldiers normally shoot at high-value targets on either side. In fact, there is an unwritten understanding among the forces on both sides that they will not shoot at helicopters—helicopters often carry senior officers. But why take a chance, he must have thought.

Having left his official vehicle behind, Noor was going about like an unidentified Pakistan Army officer along with soldiers carrying personal weapons, and 'someone' in civilian attire.

I pictured the Indian soldiers following our progress through their binoculars. Did it cross their mind to take a shot at the Pakistan patrol party? After all, they were in a position of strength there: they could shoot and get away with it. Moreover, they had no idea Noor was a brigadier, nor did they know that the 'someone' in civilian attire was an Indian.

At a time when CFVs were the order of the day, who could blame them if they took a potshot?

What would the Pakistan Army soldiers who were deputed to protect me from Indian firing be thinking? For them, at least for the moment, I might have been an Indian academic, not an enemy. They of course wouldn't shoot me while I was on their side—rather they would protect me—but if I were to be on the other side, things would have been different.

Emotions and feelings of enmity, however strong they may be, are spatio-temporally contingent. For the Indians and Pakistanis working together in other parts of the world, the need for economic coexistence trumps enmity at home. Enmity towards those you do not know, have never met and have no particular ill will against is a product of modern nationalism. Human beings have fought and killed unknown people for survival since time immemorial, but nationalism has given a new meaning to modern forms of enmity.

We drove past the jungle post and several other posts along the ridge overlooking the road, slowly, carefully and watching intently to see if there was any activity on the Indian side— not that bullets would be preceded by a warning siren. Across the elevated ridge, Pakistani posts were facing the Indian posts. Given what Noor had told me I knew that the two sides would be carefully observing each other's movements and would be ready to respond in case the need arose. They were in each other's firing range and did exchange fire during stand-offs.

What changes the equation though is not the balance of forces, posts or even weapons, but the presence of Pakistani civilian villages in the bowl between the two ridgelines atop which the Indian and Pakistani forces are perched. The Pakistani forces are on tenterhooks here because they know any misadventure from their side will have grave implications for Pakistani civilians.

Troops manning geographically 'disadvantaged' areas, therefore, have to perforce 'behave themselves' so as to not get shot by the adversary or get the civilian population shot at. Vagaries of geography often determines one's behaviour. General Tariq Waseem Ghazi once recalled an example: 'When I was commanding an area in the Poonch sector we had an area surrounded on three sides by Indian positions. We had to deliberately keep this area quiet because the slightest disturbance meant those positions would not get their reinforcements and so on, and that may also lead to other CFVs.'

Not that the Indian side would fire for the heck of it—they know that what they do in the Battal sector will have implications in other sectors. There is a 'delicate balance of terror' in operation here, to use a phrase from the American strategist Albert Wohlstetter's 1959 *Foreign Affairs* essay describing the nuclear arms race between the Cold War rivals.[2]

General Arshad pointed out during a conversation in Bangkok, on the sidelines of one of our track-II dialogues, that the location of response can be anywhere within a 200-kilometre radius of the location where the initial firing took place: 'If fired at in one area it is not necessary that you respond in the same area. If there are no good targets on the other side to respond, the brigade commander will decide to respond where we have an upper hand so we could give a better response to the other side.'

Pakistani general Yasin who was part of the conversation between me and Arshad chipped in: 'When the Indians would fire at my A post, my guy at B post would fire at the Indian side. It is the dynamic of the terrain and the tactical position. If it's a large-scale violation then you may shift it by 50 kilometres.'

In other words, firing by the Pakistan Army in the Poonch sector could potentially be responded to by the Indian Army in the Rajouri sector. This 'releasing of pressure elsewhere' dynamic could work at the brigade, battalion or even at the division level.

'You seem to be at a disadvantage here . . . so what do you do when the Indian side fires at you with no end in sight?' I asked Noor in the jeep. Despite all the tension around, he seemed to be in no hurry. He was carefully negotiating the village roads, with their occasional boulders and potholes.

'Well, we have earmarked places for retaliation not too far from here. There is a system of things on the LoC . . . nothing goes un-responded to.' Perfect symmetry, I thought to myself. Upon return, I created a website to present the data on CFVs, which included a graph to indicate the daily occurrence of CFVs. What the graph shows is indeed a perfect symmetry of firing by the Indian and Pakistani forces. Nothing goes un-responded to.

Retired Indian brigadier Arun Sahgal once explained to me the dynamics of revenge firing in these words: 'If in firing or through BAT actions or through infiltration, a battalion suffers casualties, there is no question of the battalion pulling out of the sector, without causing similar or greater damage. This is the standard rule up there . . . The unwritten law of the jungle, as far as violations are concerned, is that any provocation, any casualty by either side is always responded to.'

After close to forty minutes on the worn-out road, and under the constant gaze of the Indian and Pakistani forces, we arrived at the Tatrinote–Chakan Da Bagh trading point. Indian trucks were just about to cross over to 'our' side and to offload goods in special compounds earmarked for the purpose. The Indian drivers would be allowed to drive their trucks into the compound on the Pakistani side but would not be allowed to leave the compound.

Noor invited me to join him in the officials' gallery to watch the gate-opening ceremony. The army men manning the gate on either side stomped the ground in preparation for the opening of the gate. Once the gate was opened, there was a great deal of cordiality: smiles, handshakes and pleasantries. The two army majors acknowledged each other, the quarantine officers shook hands and Trade Facilitation Centre (TFC) personnel double-checked the lists of items. Trucks whizzed past. Pakistani trucks are way more beautiful, adorned with legendary truck art—intricate green, yellow and blue designs that add a touch of colour and pride to the otherwise simple lives of the truck drivers. Noor pointed out one particularly fancy-looking truck whose well-adorned masthead seemed to bend towards the front, like a newly-wed woman weighed down by more-than-necessary bridal jewellery. 'Look at those details,' he said with a tinge of exuberance.

'So much patience must have gone into this,' I responded. Indian trucks had nothing to show off: they just meant business.

The whole process around cross-LoC trade is detailed and time-consuming, though the trade itself is nominal, limited and based on a system of barter. No cash exchange, no banking system—only goods for goods, though the values of the goods traded is registered so that they can be made even on the balance sheets. But then cross-LoC trade is more about symbols than substance. The limited, controlled barter trade of select items between the two sides of the former princely state makes hardly any economic sense. It's the image of hope, of what's possible, and what used to happen once upon a time, seventy years ago. There are occasional allegations of narcotics trade and hawala transactions under the cover of the cross-LoC trade. 'While the traders are only allowed to trade in Kashmiri-origin items, they often source items from outside the state, in clear violation of the rules,' a police officer told me later on the Indian side.

'Well, so what? The more they trade the better,' I responded.

The officers on the Indian side looked warm and cordial and seemed to be displaying a certain amount of deference. The presence of a senior officer—a brigadier—on 'our' side seemed to have made a difference. Interestingly, it is part of the protocol that junior officers salute seniors irrespective of which side they belong to, and soldiers from the two sides refer to each other as 'your excellency'. In both Ferozepur and Wagah–Attari, the junior officers from one side take permission from seniors on the other side, if senior officers were to be present, to start the parade ceremony.

I wanted to walk up to the gate—around 20 metres from where we were seated—and say hello to the Indian Army officers (Noor told me that one of the officers on the Indian side was a major). I would have to do it from across the tall iron gate on the Pakistani side. I was fascinated by the idea of walking up to the Pakistani gate, get it opened, walk to the middle of the 'no man's land' between the two gates marked by a white line on the ground, request the Indian Army major to walk down to the 'no man's land' for a chit-chat. He might come out. I would introduce myself as an Indian academic from New Delhi. What would his response be when I say I am an Indian? Would Noor accompany me? Would the major salute the brigadier? Would the three of us share chai and pakoras? What would the conversation be like? What would the major go back and report about seeing an Indian with a Pakistani brigadier on the enemy side of the LoC? But more importantly, would they then get back to their respective sides and later start firing at each other?

I decided against making that 20-metre trip. Bit too complicated, I thought to myself.

This is a classic case of the theatre of the absurd. Consider this: the civility and cordiality between the two sides is amazing at the trading point, including how deference is shown to senior officers on the other side. The men who shake hands and call each other 'your excellency' will shoot to kill if they were a kilometre away. This was a cordon sanitaire, an area where there could be no firing, with firing breaking out all around it.

'What does your bunker look like? How about I visit one?' I asked, pointing at a close-by Pakistani post. My request was ignored.

'We will try to organize it,' was my liaison officer's response. But they never took me inside the Pakistani army post. Were they worried about making their first line of defence vulnerable to the prying eyes of an Indian? A post and a bunker on the LoC serve the crucial purpose of defending the line, initiating fire, taking cover during fire, weapon storage, etc. I had many questions to ask: How reinforced are the bunkers? Can they withstand artillery fire? What kind of weapons systems are stored there? What about the morale of the men in those bunkers? How are they compared to the Indian bunkers which I had been to some time ago? Had I made it to a Pakistani bunker or post, I would have wanted to view Indian soldiers from the Pakistani post's peephole, or through the binoculars. How do Indians look from this side, I wondered.

I never made it to a Pakistani bunker; I was kept a few hundred metres away—it was as if they foresaw my questions.

The theatre of the absurd refused to fade away from my mind even after I returned from Battal and Tatrinote.

On the night of 25 December 2017,[3] less than a week after I returned from Pakistan, a Special Forces Unit of the Indian Army crossed the LoC in the Poonch sector and killed three Pakistani soldiers, avenging Indian casualties. The area of operation was under the 2-AK brigade, close to where Noor had warned of possible 'enemy fire'. Since then there have been several reports of CFVs, casualties and injuries. The Battal sector has a special place in my heart, and it makes me sad whenever I hear of deaths and injuries in the area.

There is another reason why the Battal sector is special to me: Dharmsal village falls in the Battal sector.

'I Was Shot in the Neck'

'I was shot in the neck on 10 June 2017. I was running when the bullets came raining down, but I was hit a little short of the makeshift community bunker,' said fifteen-year-old Usman with a broad smile. Why would someone sheepishly smile when talking about getting shot by an enemy bullet? Was it the typical teenage coyness? When Usman stood up and narrated his ordeal to me, his village buddies teased him for getting shot. 'He is a real lousy runner,' one of the boys behind him said with a laugh, 'and he literally can't run to save his own life.' Usman was struggling to ignore their taunts so as to continue the conversation with me.

I knew it was silly to ask him about what went on in his mind when he was shot, but I was curious to know what it felt like to be shot at. 'The neck is a bad place to get shot. The moment the bullet pierced me, I thought it was all over. There was a sharp pain and I fell on the ground and became unconscious, more from the fall than because of the bullet. The bullet pierced the side of my neck and went through, and I survived.' He was evacuated only after the firing and the retaliatory firing were both over. The villagers took him to the army hospital and he survived. It was a morbid feeling, listening to the young boy talk about how he was shot, and how he sounded so normal, even nonchalant, describing it.

He might have described it to a hundred people by now, hence the casual approach to it. Or perhaps he was just being a frisky youngster.

He wasn't the only survivor. There were several who narrated their stories and showed me their bullet/shrapnel scars. 'We know our fauj will avenge us,' I was told again and again.

Then there were older men, bearded and pensive, who insisted that revenge would not help their problems. It would bring more shells, they reasoned. The agitated younger lot didn't like those words of wisdom; they murmured disapprovingly.

In this shooting war between Indian and Pakistani armed forces, civilians are the hapless victims. They get shot at, killed, their livestock injured/killed, houses destroyed and harvests damaged. In the first three months of 2018 alone, around twenty-five Pakistani civilians lost their lives, as did thirteen Indian civilians.[4]

I was seated on the terrace of the village sarpanch's house to take in the afternoon warmth of the December sun. The house was within the firing range of Indian and Pakistani troops. The village was located on the mountain slope right under the nose of the Indian posts and was visible to the Pakistani posts on the other side. The freshly painted houses were riddled with bullet marks, and the terrace walls had several huge holes drilled in by Indian shells. Milk tea, freshly fried pakoras and other savouries were served to the guests. Young kids looked eagerly at the refreshments, awaiting their turn. Noor and I sat in the middle and the elderly men from the village sat around us, with the younger ones standing, and the womenfolk confined to their homes. Younger girls peeped through openings in the window. Most of the village had gathered to talk to the man from the enemy side—some to complain and vent, some to request for peace and some to just meet me and Brigadier Noor. There was a sense of urgency in the air, and a feeling of being embattled.

Armed Pakistani army soldiers stood around the edges of the terrace to watch out for any unprovoked Indian action. They kept chatting on their walkie-talkies with their colleagues, who were keeping a watch on the Indians, in the bunkers on the hills opposite.

'Indian' bullets and unexploded shells were amply displayed right in the middle of the circle. Anecdotes about the Indian atrocities were also in abundance. The older men recalled the days before the fence, in the 1980s, when they would cross back and forth into the Indian side. Nobody would bother. Occasional shooting would take place, but things were never this bad. 'It was in the 1990s that firing started getting really bad and wreaked havoc in the border villages.' The older generation sounded nostalgic about India, and the Indians and Kashmiris living a few kilometres away. 'They are family . . . our brothers and sisters. When our army retaliates, it's our own family members who die,' was their impassioned plea.

'Please tell your army when you go back that they should have a war with the Pakistan Army and end the matter once and for all. We don't want this low-intensity war happening on a daily basis. Our cattle get killed, our people are crippled, our kids can't go to school. How long will we continue with this subhuman existence?' That was a desperate plea, and I didn't quite know what to say.

'I hope there will be peace between the two countries. We are all heavily invested in peace,' I responded. They had heard such statements before, and I think they realized I just didn't have any hope to give out.

'Sure, but for the people in the cities, peace is big talk. For us, peace is about not getting killed, it's as real as it can get,' said someone, countering me. I didn't know what to say except to agree with it. How true: for most of my ilk, peace is desirable—it's virtuous, liberal, modern and an enlightened way of life; for the people of Dharmsal, and many such villages on either side of the line, it's simply about not getting killed by a bullet or shrapnel. It's about staying alive on a day-to-day basis. They must know the value of staying alive. They must know death so intimately so as to talk about it with such stoic abandon.

Life on the LoC is like living in front of a firing squad, that's in no hurry—a firing squad that has orders to shoot at you, but it decides against immediately carrying out those orders. It takes its time, patiently observes you, enjoys your fear, occasionally sprays bullets in the vicinity and turns the other way when you run for cover. When you settle down, they fire at you again. Some of your friends die, some get hurt, but you have no choice but to continue to live before the firing squad, exposed to their guns. You are vulnerable to their whims, fancies and mood swings. If that's not brutal enough, imagine two rival firing squads on opposite sides and you caught between them furiously firing at each other, for reasons best known to them. Members of the firing squads change every now and then, and as a result they hardly empathize with your plight. Your idea of peace is like a moody spell of good weather that comes and goes at will, limited to the interregnum between showers of bullets.

'Do you sometimes cross over to meet your family on the other side?' I asked.

'We used to but not any more. There is a risk of getting shot. But on occasions some of them come here on the three-month-visit permit,' one said, referring to the three-month travel permit given to Kashmiris to travel to the other side to meet their relatives. While the travel permit has created some enthusiasm among villagers about being able to meet their relatives, there are also complaints of security agencies hassling the visitors while on the other side and after they return home.

'How do you live here? Have you ever considered shifting out? Moving to a new village where Indian shells won't reach you?' I asked, knowing fully well that it was a rhetorical question.

'We were born here, it's our ancestral land, we will die here some day,' a bearded old man spoke up with a sense of honour and nostalgia, and pain. 'More so,' he continued, 'our forefathers are buried around here.'

'Where will we go even if we wanted to? Who will give us land?' murmured a younger chap seated behind the bearded man. That sounded more realistic.

The realization that I was in a war zone suddenly took hold of me. Scary tales of daily firing, heart-rending accounts of deaths and injuries, and routine damage to habitats. Most houses had bullet marks and shell damage to the walls. Injured people walking about, some with bullets lodged inside their bodies. A makeshift community bunker to which people ran in case of sustained firing. And yet, here they were, gathered around me, someone from the enemy country, to tell their stories and treat me with tea and pakoras. At that point in time, I would have understood if they resented my presence there. I represented the enemy, but they chose to see me beyond the shades of friendship and enmity.

The tragedy of having to choose between near-assured poverty and potential death sounded Kafkaesque to me. Once you know that you have nowhere to go, the human mind does what it does best: it fabricates a solid rationale for being there, creates mental barricades around it and justifies it. Man/woman has the unenviable ability to make peace with

the worst of his/her circumstances and be reproduced by it—
the quintessential human predicament.

J&K, unlike Punjab, was not divided by Cyril Radcliffe in
1947. The artificial divisions in J&K and the divided families
are a result of the 1947–48 war, and to some extent the 1971
war when some villages were further divided as part of the
post-war settlement. The 1965 war witnessed action in J&K,
but the territorial status quo was maintained after the end of
the war.

I was taken to the local school in the village, a building right
in the heart of the bowl between the two highly militarized
mountaintops, occupied by the Indian and Pakistani armies.
The almost-charred building had had its concrete roof blown
off, and was burnt in several places due to shelling. Bullet-
sized peepholes riddled the blackened walls. Being a teacher,
I realize the importance of education and what could happen
to children if they don't get an education. It's tragic.

It was heartening to see that even in the face of adversity,
schoolteachers organized classes in the damaged building.
Or in the front yard, in clear view of Indian soldiers perched
on top of the mountain, perhaps leaving the choice to them,
whether to fire or not, appealing to their humanity.

At JNU, we often hold classes in the open in order to
protest against the high-handedness of the administration.
We do so to protest, thereby making a political choice. The
villagers on the LoC don't have the agency to make such
choices. They are victims of someone else's agency and choice.

Does the firing side—India or Pakistan—realize what
their bullets do to habitats and human beings just 800 metres
below their posts? These are people whom the shooters have
never met, will never meet and yet consider enemies. I guess
the soldiers know what happens when they fire, because it
happens on their side too.

Is there a way that school buildings could be painted differently so as to identify them such that they could be spared the shelling? Even better, could there be some sort of a cordon sanitaire for the hapless villagers, their cattle and their kids, where they could run to when shells and bullets descend on them? Unlikely, for these people are the victims of the hyper-nationalism being beamed into the living rooms of our safe, secure urban homes. They atone for our sins. There is a sophisticated phrase for it in modern military terminology: collateral damage. Collateral damage is the phrase you invoke when you have to wash off the sins of having killed innocents, and be able to sleep at night.

While on a field visit to the Bhimber Gali brigade near the LoC on the Indian side of Kashmir, I heard eyewitness accounts of the death of Karamat Hussain—the head of Bala Kote village on the LoC—who was killed along with six others while travelling in a car which was hit by a Pakistani 120-mm shell. The firing by Pakistan took place on the Indian Independence day in 2015. Hussain's house was not in the range of the Pakistani mortar shells, but he was hit while en route home. When I met his teenage daughter, she hoped that the Indian Army teaches the Pakistanis a lesson for killing her father. 'I didn't get enough of my father's love,' she said heart-rendingly.

Curiously, Noor had left about half an hour before I had begun my journey from the brigade HQ to Dharmsal village in the Battal sector. He was engaged in a serious conversation with the men from the village on the terrace by the time I got there. Had he been telling them what to tell me? Had he been making sure that they didn't tell me what they shouldn't? Given that the sector was a highly sensitive one, I wouldn't be surprised if that were the case.

Out of necessity and habit, both the Indian and Pakistani armies keep a close watch on the population on their respective sides, ensuring, perhaps, that they don't engage in any undesirable activities, or perhaps because the armies and the security agencies would like to keep total control over these border populations. In any case, border populations live under the binocular gaze of armed men perched in the hilltops along the LoC.

Then there are mines. During a visit to the border in Uri with the Indian Army, not far from the civilian habitats, I was strictly asked to move behind soldiers carrying mine detectors so that I don't accidentally step on a stray mine. The man leading the troops swung the detector from left to right. Two armed soldiers were a few feet behind him and I was right at the back. With nature's progress, the deep undergrowth will have hidden a number of mines too well for the human eye to detect, hence the precautions. The possibility of there being drifted, and therefore unsecured, mines along the outskirts of the villages was not ruled out by the officers I spoke to. There is a lot of undergrowth in the areas close to the LoC and the IB in Jammu, and it is possible that such areas would have drifted mines. This is because practical considerations and prohibitive costs make the task of demining an area a difficult one.

Both India and Pakistan use anti-personnel landmines on the LoC and sometimes even on the IB or working boundary (WB) as Pakistan refers to the border in Jammu, like in the Samba sector in Jammu. Mines were placed across the India–Pakistan border area in 1947, 1965, 1971 and again in 2001 during Operation Parakram. Some of those old mines continue to remain in place. Sites with mines are marked and safeguarded with fences and meshes as per Protocol-II of the Geneva Convention of 1980. Sometimes these mines drift away from the meshed areas due to environmental factors, and there have been several mine-related accidents. Sometimes rains wash away both the mines and the mesh, making the management of mines difficult.

Villagers and their livestock often become victims of drifted mines. The result is loss of life and limb, and suffering. A landmine monitor report estimates that around 2 million mines were laid from December 2001 to mid-2002. Around 16,000 acres of land in the Jammu region and 1,73,000 acres in Kashmir were also reportedly mined during this period.[5] While the Indian government claims that almost all of this area has been demined, officials on the ground say that a lot of mines continue to remain in place and have killed hundreds of civilians and soldiers. A report published by the Landmine and Cluster Munition Monitor showed that 1074 people were killed and 2068 were injured by the end of 2012 in J&K in mine-related incidents.[6] The Government of India stated in Parliament in 2004 that during the period from 1 January 2002 to 30 November 2002, forty-eight civilians were killed and 236 were injured in landmine blasts in the three states bordering Pakistan, namely Rajasthan, Punjab and J&K. From 1 January 2000 to 30 April 2002, the government stated in the Parliament that 138 army personnel were killed in mine or improvised explosive devices (IED)–related accidental blasts. While most of the mines were removed, officials posted in these areas say that these areas have not been fully demined.

India and Pakistan have conspicuously not signed the 1997 Ottawa convention, more formally the 'Convention on the Prohibition of the Use, Stockpiling, Production and Transfer of Anti-Personnel Mines and on Their Destruction'.

Dharmsal was about humanizing statistics, meeting and listening to the people who were hidden away behind the official data points. At the end of my visit to the village I understood why there was a sheepish smile on the fifteen-year-old Usman's face when he described how he was shot at. It was probably not a 'big deal' to get shot in that village.

Violence is so normal in Dharmsal that making a 'big fuss' about getting shot is almost laughable to its inhabitants.

Where the Jhelum and Neelum Clash

The river Neelum, also called the Kishanganga, originates in the Indian side of J&K and flows into the Pakistani side. So does the Jhelum, originating in the Pir Panjal mountain range on the Indian side, and eventually sneaking into the enemy territory. They join forces near Muzaffarabad, the capital city of Pakistan-occupied Kashmir. The 1-AK brigade (or 1-PoK brigade, as the Indian side refers to it) HQ is bang on the banks of their confluence.

Brigadier Akhtar Khan and I were on a late-evening stroll along the banks of the river Jhelum, not too far from where the Neelum crashed into it. 'This is an unbeatable view; the serenity here is only broken by the deadly noise of shells exploding at a distance.' Akhtar, the short, bearded, talkative chief of the brigade sounded poignant for a moment. Akhtar's gunman followed us at a distance, just in case, I guessed.

He was right. With the dusk upon us, birds chirping, darkness slowly enveloping the scene, and the gurgling sound of the river Jhelum, the walk was indeed a memorable one. It was a cold mid-December evening, and our walk and talk had just begun. The HQ is on a mountain slope, a few hundred kilometres below the hilltop where the PC chain has a new hotel. The brigade HQ's well-manicured lawns and garden were highlighted by high-mast lighting poles. Armed men stood at various points in the compound, staring into the empty darkness around them.

Akhtar Khan is a talkative man, and he can speak on any subject with ease, especially on the LoC and Kashmir—he mans a crucial stretch on the LoC with India. Azad Kashmir regiments of the Pakistan Army have been manning the LoC (previously called the Cease-Fire Line or CFL from 1948 to 1972) since the outbreak of the first war between India and Pakistan in 1947 over J&K.

Unlike the other officers I had met, Akhtar speaks fast, fervently, wears a smile and has an almost missionary zeal. I imagined he would have been a preacher had he not joined the army. It was as if he had made it his mission to impress me rather than to merely show me around. Earlier that evening, he had taken me to show me a burnt-down bus. 'It was hit by an Indian shell, killing everyone inside it instantly,' he had pointed out. The bus, hit by an Indian shell on 23 November 2016 in Nagader Lawat Neelum, not only displayed posters of the unfortunate people who were killed but also the pictures of some of the separatist leaders in the Indian Kashmir. Among the pictures that adorned the bus were those of Mirwaiz Umar Farooq, Kashmir's chief priest and chairman of the All Parties Hurriyat Conference (APHC), and the late People's Conference leader Abdul Ghani Lone, the father of Sajjad Lone, a former minister in the J&K government.

'Take a photograph, if you want to,' he had said encouragingly. I was pleasantly surprised.

There was a reason for my surprise. I was summarily discouraged from taking photographs while in PoK. There was no question of recording conversations with anyone on the other side. These were clear instructions. Very interestingly, the lower-ranking officers and soldiers largely kept away from me. The story on the other side was different: I could photograph whatever I pleased, and I could also talk to anyone and everyone I could find while travelling with the Indian Army. I mingled with the Indian rank and file and would get into an army bunker and have chai and pakoras with great ease. The Indian officials and soldiers encouraged it. Not so on the Pakistani side. I had to be mindful of certain limits. But that was understandable.

I continued to irritate them for a local SIM card. How could I survive four days without access to Internet? That was almost the first thing I had told the colonel when I had arrived at the Islamabad airport. In his typical style, he had said he would look into it. That evening itself, I reminded him at least four times about it. And yet it only arrived when I got to Muzaffarabad on the evening of the following day. And even then it was not data-enabled. It took them another two hours to get the data issue fixed. By the time I had data in my phone, we were in the border areas where access to the Internet was close to impossible.

* * *

'Brigadier Khan is a few years junior to me,' the colonel told me. That made sense. I was puzzled by the exchange between them when I had walked into Brigadier Akhtar Khan's room that evening. The colonel stood at attention and gave a smart salute to the brigadier, as should be the case. And then, all of a sudden, the brigadier stood up and told him, 'Sir, please sit down,' before turning to greet me. The exchange was quick, and I would have almost missed it except that I had made it a point to notice everything that went on around me.

'What was that about? Was the brigadier pulling your leg or something by calling you "sir" and treating you with so much respect?' I later asked the colonel.

'He is my junior. I didn't make the next rank, and he was promoted over me. I salute him as he is my superior officer now, and he calls me "sir" because that's what he did until recently,' he explained.

'How does it feel to have to salute your junior officer?' I pressed on.

'Well, these are army customs and one gets used to them.' He didn't seem particularly distraught about it.

* * *

Akhtar Khan's brigade not only mans the LoC, but also facilitates the activities on the cross-LoC trading point at Chakothi. Indian Army officers say that he is also in charge of training terrorists and facilitating their infiltration into J&K. He, according to Indian sources, is one of the Pakistan Army's key men in charge of operations in J&K. He, of course, has a different view about what happens in Kashmir.

Walking along the riverbank, I was acutely aware that I was on a piece of territory that has had a deep impact on India–Pakistan relations. The first war between the newly independent countries was fought along those very tracts of land.

What would Indo-Pak relations have been like today were it not for those thousands of tribesmen and Pakistan Army regulars who, on 22 October 1947, had reached the spot where Akhtar and I were taking our evening stroll? I wondered. What if the Indian government had rushed troops to Kashmir a few weeks earlier when the first request from the maharaja of J&K, Hari Singh, had arrived in New Delhi on 1 October 1947 and the Indian government had been able to send weapons and men to Kashmir? Would this land have been a part of the Indian side of J&K?

On the other hand, what if General Sir Douglas David Gracey, the then chief of army staff of Pakistan, had actually carried out Jinnah's orders to march to Kashmir? What if he had not threatened Jinnah about issuing stand-down orders to his men? What would have been the fate of this territory? Would Pakistan be in custody of more land than it has today? What would have happened if historical events had turned out differently?

Well, things didn't turn out differently and here we are, doing everything we can to safeguard the status quo of 1948 (for the most part), frozen in time, as it were—fighting to preserve the past rather than striving for a new future.

'We are all worried about the human rights violations in Kashmir.' Akhtar's voice broke my chain of 'what if' thoughts.

'Part of what happens is because of your work, brigadier,' I said with a laugh. He carefully avoided responding to my allusion to Pakistan's support for armed militancy in Kashmir, nor did he seem amused. He was keener to focus on 'freedom fighters', who in his opinion were fighting the might of the Indian state on their own in Kashmir.

'It's their legitimate struggle for self-determination; we have nothing to do with it.' He was emphatic.

His counterparts in J&K would argue the exact opposite: that everything that happens in Kashmir is a result of what the Pakistan Army or ISI does; that they recruit, train and arm rebel groups and help them infiltrate J&K; that these rebels fight on behalf of Pakistan and are terrorists, not freedom fighters. The truth lies somewhere in the middle, one could say. But I didn't press the point.

What caught my attention was his mention of the fact that Kashmiris travel to either side rather effortlessly. Someone else who I met earlier that evening had confirmed this as well.

Akhtar was also keen to impress upon me that he only ordered firing in retaliation, just as the Indian side would convince me that it was always retaliatory fire. 'Almost never,'

he said, 'would we fire without provocation by your side,'—
an argument that sits in direct contradiction to what 'my side'
had told me. Again, a researcher should be able to tell when
someone is being charitable with the truth.

'We have always looked at India as a threat,' he said,
repeating what several others in the Pakistan Army had told me.
'Sure, it's a feeling, but not one without historical basis. Look at
how India was never serious about a plebiscite in Kashmir. And
shouldn't we be concerned about a dominant neighbour which
cut our country into two?' Note that the latter is a legitimate
argument, notwithstanding the pressing circumstances under
which India intervened in East Pakistan to create Bangladesh.
Moreover, most Indians seem to be oblivious of what that
victory did to Pakistan, physically and psychologically.

The country got truncated, pure and simple. But more
importantly, it was a humiliating experience for a country
that always reeled under a sense of inferiority before India.
Many of the young Pakistani army officers who surrendered
before India in 1971 went on to occupy leadership positions
in the Pakistan Army. Memories of humiliation, of national
humiliation, generate a culture of resentment and rivalry.
'1971' is a constant refrain among the rank and file of the
Pakistan military. 'But even the youngest officer who was
part of the Pakistan Army during the 1971 war must have
retired from active service a long time ago. Why is the defeat
of seventy-one still a big deal for the Pakistan Army?' I asked
a retired Pakistani general on the sidelines of one of our track-
II meetings.

'True it was long time ago, but stories of humiliation
and the need to extract revenge are handed down through
generations. It's part of our collective memory,' he responded.
So those Indians who ask 'Why does the Pakistan Army hate
us?' need to be more historically sensitive.

'But make no mistake, we are prepared to defend ourselves, we will fight till death,' Akhtar added quickly, lest I get back to India with the feeling that the Pakistan Army is weak. The India focus of the Pakistan Army is not unknown. In fact, many analysts even argue that the bogey that is India is a major raison d'être of the Pakistan Army's domestic legitimacy.

I recalled the conversation with a Pakistani colonel during that trip. India looms large in the Pakistani military imagination: from basic training to war games to exercises, India figures in everything. And yet the understanding of India is inadequate and complicated. For many Pakistanis, India is a Hindu and internally divided country without a clear sense of purpose. Looking at the manner in which our domestic politics has been vitiated by radical Hindutva ideology in recent years, one might say there is some truth to it. And yet, India continues to be a country that celebrates its plural culture and secular ethos.

Akhtar and I ended our walk along the river. We would not be meeting each other again as I would head out for Rawalakot early morning on the following day. I shook his hands and thanked him for his hospitality. 'Let's hope there will be an end to this violence soon,' I said. He smiled and wished me good night.

'Inshallah, We Will Prevail'

'Inshallah, we will prevail.' I was a bit taken aback when a senior Pakistani army officer said this while discussing Indo-Pak rivalry and the balance of forces between the two adversaries. I would have dismissed it as a routine recourse to a cultural idiom, except for his constant references to Koranic invocations on victory, success and war. Not that I followed the meaning of any of that, but in all my years of talking to Indian and Pakistani army officers, I have never heard an Indian Army officer quoting from the Hindu, Islamic or Sikh religious texts. I sometimes come across, though not frequently, Pakistani officers who make religious references right in the middle of factual and logical discussions on statecraft and warfare. It's not often that one comes across Pakistani officers who consume alcoholic drinks. The consumption of alcoholic drinks is not necessarily an indication of a liberal outlook, but then abstinence would potentially indicate a higher degree of religiosity. And again, higher degrees of religiosity do not necessarily mean lower levels of military competence.

Many Pakistanis are genuinely confused about the role of other religions and those who profess them in a country like India.

I met a civilian bureaucrat in Brigadier Akhtar Khan's office late one evening after the riverside stroll. The woman bureaucrat, the refugee commissioner based in the provincial capital, Muzaffarabad, was invited to give me a broad-brush picture of the Kashmiri refugees from India living on their side. According to the young, articulate officer, around 38,000 Kashmiri refugees, or around 7000 families, currently live in PoK. While they went to PoK in several phases, most of them went there during the late 1980s when the Kashmir insurgency began. Some have gone back (perhaps to fight the Indian state, she didn't say that), some have stayed back and settled down there and some might return in future.

There is a full and complete denial when it comes to the question of terrorism and militant infiltration into J&K. When repeatedly asked whether the Kashmiri refugee population in PoK travel back and forth to India, the refugee commissioner answered: 'We don't stop the Kashmiris—how can we? But we don't encourage it either.'

In any case, local propaganda in PoK about Kashmir is exceptionally strong. Talk to anyone, and the first few sentences will be on Kashmir and Kashmiris, along expected lines. Their general position is that there is a struggle for self-determination in Kashmir and that the Indian state is carrying out an ethnic cleansing there; that Kashmir needs to be resolved according to the UN Security Council's resolutions; and that there is a struggle for independence in Kashmir.

I would often ask, 'But how can Kashmir be independent? Certainly not on the basis of the UN's resolutions since they do not provide for independence.' In response, I was mostly met with blank looks.

'You are a Christian!' said the bureaucrat, puzzled. India's religious pluralism is a mystery to many Pakistanis, and that's why I correct them when they say 'Hindustan'. To me, one fundamental difference between India and Pakistan has always been the public display of religiosity in the two countries. In India, I think religion is far less excruciatingly invasive of our private space and spiritual choices. Let me explain. In India, you have control over your individual preferences for religion. In India, religion needn't define you, unless you choose to let it. Of course, the Indian public discourse and public spaces are increasingly getting shaped by religion and its dogmas, especially those of Hinduism. But religion continues to be an option in the country.

In Pakistan, religion is unmissably evident in the public space, and I as an individual have little choice in terms of avoiding it. Whether or not you like it, you have to come to terms with it. Religion, in Pakistan, often is not an option.

So when the bureaucrat exclaimed that I was Christian, I knew the source of her puzzlement, a feeling that is generated by exposure to the predominance of one religion. Everything gets viewed through the predetermined lens of Islam and

Islamic teachings. 'I am,' I said, and made it a point to tell her what I thought of religion: 'I don't let it make a difference to my life or my world view.' That was one way of telling her that I was an atheist.

That said, I would not make a value judgement on whether or not faith helps in winning wars—I do not know. What does military morale depend on besides bravado, valour, patriotism and a sense of duty? Do repeated utterances of 'inshallah' lead to its literal meaning having a subconscious impact on the behaviour of the men? Does religion contribute in some measure to an army's morale? I guess anything could? The difference of course is that religion is far more than an abstract value, and it can complicate the workings of organizational structures way more than an abstract idea can do.

Military organizations are also home to regimented belief systems, and there have been occasions when religious beliefs have informed the Pakistan Army's views about India. Two related examples from history readily come to mind. Mohammad Ayub Khan, Pakistan's army chief in the early 1950s and the country's president for eleven years from the late 1950s to the late 1960s, has been quoted by Altaf Gauhar in his book *Ayub Khan: Pakistan's First Military Ruler* as having said that 'as a general rule, Hindu morale would not stand more than a couple of hard blows at the right time and place' and that one Muslim soldier was 'worth ten Hindus'.[7] His expectations were dashed during the 1965 war when the course and outcome of the war were determined by balance of forces and strategic planning, and not by the religious doctrines professed by the men who fought the war.

In any case, the presence of this interesting cultural factor does not take away from the fact that the Pakistan Army is an exceptionally professional force: religious, India-centric and ruthlessly trained. Given the fact that both the armies had the same historical origin and the morals, training and traditions that go with it, there is not much of a difference between the standard operating procedures and operational cultures of the two rival armies. And yet, their world views are drastically different. The Pakistan Army has a revisionist world view that sits uneasily with the diktats of the status quo, making it an aggressive force. The Indian Army, the status quoist one, has a defensive mindset.

On the LoC itself, the rank and file of the Pakistan Army maintain a very high morale, and are battle-hardened thanks to the counter-insurgency operations in the Khyber Pakhtunkhwa (KP) province. But their upbeat morale is not matched by the material conditions on the ground. The army has shallow deployments both in terms of men and defence constructions. The Pakistani side has not erected border fences, has stationed fewer troops, constructed fewer posts and carries out very little patrolling along the zero line. As a result, India has a clear infrastructural superiority, in numerical terms, over the Pakistani side. The Indian side of the LoC is manned by two (XV and XVI) corps and six battalions of the BSF, whereas the Pakistani side has just two divisions (23 and 12) under the Rawalpindi corps manning the LoC, of which the 23rd division has four brigades and the 12 division has six brigades. This is clearly no match for the overwhelming Indian might on the LoC.

While it is true that in the day-to-day management of the LoC, morale, or 'moral ascendency' as the armies call it, matters a great deal, numerical and material superiority will come to bear when there is a sustained offensive operation. In other words, numerical inferiority could lead to a potential inability to hold territory in case the Indian side decides to grab posts or carry out surgical strikes, etc.

The Lonely Peacekeepers

'Meet the man whose job it is to keep peace between us,' said Brigadier Noor, introducing to me a major from the United Nations Military Observer Group in India and Pakistan (UNMOGIP). The Scandinavian army officer wearing a blue UN cap saluted him. I had requested my hosts to introduce me to the UNMOGIP group located at the Rawalakot brigade's HQ. I had never met UNMOGIP officials before, and so I was keen to have a conversation with them. We were setting out from Noor's office to go to the forward posts when we came across the major and I immediately grabbed the opportunity to have a conversation with the officer. The major seemed keen to talk as well. Perhaps he was bored of one of the UN's most thankless 'peacekeeping' missions.

UNMOGIP was set up on the recommendation of the United Nations Commission for India and Pakistan (UNCIP) which was mandated by the 1948 Security Council Resolution 39 to investigate and mediate the dispute between India and Pakistan over Kashmir. It helped maintain relative peace between the sides, except during war, till 1971.

However, following the Simla Agreement of 1972, India maintained 'that the mandate of UNMOGIP had lapsed, since its mandate related specifically to the ceasefire line under the Karachi Agreement. Pakistan, however, did not accept this position.' Pakistan continued 'to lodge complaints with UNMOGIP about ceasefire violations', whereas 'the military authorities of India have lodged no complaints since January 1972 and have restricted the activities of the UN observers on the Indian side of the Line of Control'.

The primary function of UNMOGIP is investigation and observation: to 'observe and report, investigate complaints of ceasefire violations and submit its finding to each party and to the Secretary-General'.[8] Prior to 1971, if a CFV occurred, a UNMOGIP team would go to the location to investigate the violation. The request for investigation, however, had to come from either the Indian or the Pakistani side. After 1971, while Pakistan continued to request investigation into violations, India stopped doing so. The UNMOGIP investigation reports are kept confidential and are only given to the UN HQ.

India has been discouraging UNMOGIP's work in the region. The country's new government under Narendra Modi, for instance, had asked UNMOGIP in 2014 to vacate the government building used as its office in New Delhi since India considers that the utility of the group is long over. Moreover, two Indian Army personnel are usually present at the UNMOGIP office in New Delhi, seeking information from visitors about the nature and reason of their visit to the UNMOGIP office—which is unusual for a UN office.

A UNMOGIP official in New Delhi pointed out that there is a lot of restriction on UNMOGIP's movement in India. Any meeting that UNMOGIP seeks to organize, professional or personal, requires tedious clearances from the military and civilian bureaucracy in India. This, the official pointed out, is in complete contrast to the great amount of freedom enjoyed by UNMOGIP in Islamabad to meet political and military leaders there. A brigadier-level officer from the Pakistan Army acts as the liaison officer for UNMOGIP to help establish contact with the political and military leadership in Pakistan.

Over the years, New Delhi has tried to de-emphasize the role of the UNMOGIP and has made its functioning difficult in J&K. UNMOGIP officials are not allowed to visit any of the operational areas on the Indian side of the LoC and IB. They are supposed to inform the Indian Army about their travel and visit schedule in advance, and they have an Indian

Army driver to take them around, which further increases the Indian government's control over the functioning of the group. The UNMOGIP vehicles pass from India into Pakistan only through the Octroi Border Outpost, located in Jammu around 11 kilometres away from Pakistan's Sialkot. The post was established by the British as a pre-Independence railway line and tax-collection point for trade between Jammu and Punjab. However, there was a time when UNMOGIP was not only welcome in the region but, more importantly, played a crucial role in resolving many disputes between India and Pakistan in J&K.

There is of course a certain logic behind India's inhospitable behaviour: India does not want to recognize, and therefore legitimize, the work of the UN group—and yet, India has not written formally to the United Nations Security Council (UNSC) to withdraw UNMOGIP from J&K. Doing so, it knows, would open a Pandora's box on the Kashmir question, which it knows best to avoid. For instance, an official Indian request to the UNSC to withdraw UNMOGIP will trigger a series of discussions and debates within the SC on Kashmir, potentially including the issue of plebiscite.

I asked the Scandinavian major what procedure UNMOGIP followed on the Pakistani side. Upon receiving a complaint of CFVs by India from the Pakistan Army, UNMOGIP officials would verify protest and inform the HQ in New York. On occasion, they would pitch a tent to stay in the forward areas. When travelling to hot areas, they make sure that they are clearly identifiable from the other side so as not to get caught in the crossfire. They don't investigate all complaints filed by the Pakistani side, thanks primarily to the sheer lack of personnel and the huge number of violations.

'We are free to move around here, unlike on the Indian side,' the major told me, sounding almost as if he was frustrated by the restrictions on the Indian side.

'Kashmiris Do Not Recognize the LoC'

'Do you let the local villagers go to the other side?' I asked Brigadier Akhtar Khan since I knew that the unauthorized border-crossing by civilians often triggered firing between the two sides.

'We discourage them, but they don't recognize the artificial LoC. You may build a fence, but they live their lives around these areas,' he said.

Retired Pakistani brigadier Naeem Salik once told me: 'On the Pakistani side, the civilian population is right on the zero line and sometimes even ahead of the forward post. Sometimes people cross inadvertently—they might go after cattle that runs across. People would go across to attend marriages and come back. People familiar with the territory can easily bypass despite the difficult terrain.'

But then the Indian troops who fire at unauthorized crossers can't be blamed either, since sometimes such people could be guides (to militants/infiltrators) in the garb of grazers. In any case, in times of high levels of infiltration, it is not possible to determine who is a genuine villager chasing after his cattle and who is an infiltrator hiding an AK-47.

Noor, Akhtar Khan and Azhar Abbas talked about several causes of CFVs. They said that since the Pakistani side doesn't do any defence construction along the LoC, there is no question of it being a trigger. When the Indian side makes constructions, the Pakistani army issues warnings.

'How about when the Indians make repairs to their fence which often falls within the restricted 500 yards?' I asked Akhtar.

'Then we fire. And they fire back,' he said.

Major General Azhar Abbas stressed the importance of understanding the underlying political dynamics that cause CFVs. He specifically referred to what he believed as a policy direction from the new government in New Delhi to fire at the Pakistani posts. This feeling was echoed by brigadiers Akhtar Khan and Noor, and the chief of general staff of the Pakistan Army, Lieutenant General Bilal Akbar, at the GHQ of the Pakistan military in Rawalpindi. Brigadier Akhtar Khan stated that the Indian Army fires at the Pakistani side to deflect attention from the insurgency in Kashmir, an argument strongly agreed to by Brigadier Noor.

Pakistani officers admit that the cross-LoC trade has great support among the local Kashmiri population. Even though I had arrived really late in Muzaffarabad, he made it a point to take me to the Chakothi trading point to show me standard operating procedures relating to cross-LoC trade. We drove to the Chakothi trading point under a thick blanket of darkness.

'Welcome to Chakothi, Azad Jammu and Kashmir,' said the trade commissioner of the state, welcoming me to the facility. Had he emphasized the word 'Azad'? I wondered. After a tour of the facility, accompanied by Akhtar, his entourage and the trade officials, we sat down with the local traders.

The colonel, my travel companion in PoK, sat behind me, facing the traders. The traders often made strong arguments about the Indian atrocities on the LoC and their insensitivities while carrying out the trade, and looked at the colonel as if asking if they had done well. There was, however, unanimity on what the trade has been able to do for the Kashmiris and how it has made them more hopeful about the future. 'We lose our lives, but at least now we are able to visit our family on the other side, and occasionally they come here.' Between 2005 and 2017, 5360 Indian Kashmiris crossed over to the other side to meet their relatives, and 9482 crossed to the Indian side, at the Chakothi–Uri crossing point alone.[9] The total number of Indian and Pakistani crossings from all four crossing points is 14,016 and 22,649, respectively.

'The Indian side highly restricts the number of tradable items on the list,' the traders complained. I asked the trade commissioner later if that was true. 'Well, traders do not always understand the technicalities and in their enthusiasm for more, they exaggerate their claims. There is a mutually-agreed [-upon] list of items and neither side unilateral[ly] shrinks the list,' he responded.

5

Inside the Rawalpindi Garrison

The Pathan Soldier

One would expect a liberal dose of subservience and docility when army soldiers meet their senior officers. But the interaction between the lowly soldier and the colonel sitting by my side in the army vehicle left me both puzzled and amazed. The tall, bearded, well-built Pathan guard, wearing a bulletproof vest, with what looked like an AK-47 slung across his broad chest looked unfriendly and cold when he stiffly saluted the colonel. 'Assalamualaikum,' he said in a coarse, surly voice. The colonel was in his khaki uniform, with the insignia on it stating loud and clear that he was a mid-level officer of the Pakistan Army. The guard couldn't have missed that, but the presence of a colonel made no difference to the man guarding gate number 1 of the Pakistan Army's GHQ in Rawalpindi. The Pathan guard looked grimly into the car, carefully scanned the occupants, stared at me for a few seconds longer, and told the colonel, who was several ranks above him: 'All of you may sit inside the car . . . You will not come out of the car under any circumstances . . . I will make a call, and someone will soon arrive to pick you up.' The driver was asked with even more terseness to turn the engine off.

There was no doubt that he was expecting us and he knew who had arrived at the gate. It made no difference to him anyhow. No smile, no semblance of subservience, no sense of insecurity—he seemed cocksure and his demeanour, almost bordering on arrogance. It was as if he took a certain pride in being boorish. Had it not been for the colonel sitting next to me and the armed guards behind me, I would have been deeply worried. I was a bit nervous despite their presence.

The stiff salute and the pinpoint precision with which he checked out the car and its passengers had me impressed. Whenever I met a guard at any military installation, I would be reminded of the strong-willed image of the Pathan soldier. Despite his low rank, I could see he took pride in his job. This was his little area of jurisdiction and everything had to be done his way. He almost made me rethink my disagreement with the British-manufactured 'martial race' in which certain ethnic, religious, caste and social groups were regarded as possessing the necessary characteristics and were therefore suited for military service.

I was equally intrigued that the colonel didn't seem to bother either—someone of his rank would normally be unhappy with such cold treatment and lack of deference from a lower-ranking man, especially in the presence of a civilian from the enemy country. Didn't the colonel consider that I might think that the soldier didn't respect him enough? When I whispered my thoughts to him, he responded with remarkable calm that the guard was merely being professional: 'That's how it should be. He would be in trouble if he doesn't do what he is doing. We've trained them that way.' Those were, according to the colonel, standard operating procedures laid down to secure the first line of defence at the Pakistan Army's highest seat of power. The guards there were trained to be cold, tough and impersonal. A few minutes ago, tough-looking armed guards had directed our driver to park in a particular space. Another burly fellow slowly circled our vehicle with an inspection mirror. A third guard stood at a distance with a sniffer dog you wouldn't want to meet in a lonely alley.

The Pathan guard went up to a cabin to make a call from the landline. I could see him through the cabin glass—not once did he relax as he made the phone call. Tall, well-built guards stood facing the street, observing the passing vehicles. They were as still as statues, and the only sign of movement could be found in their eyes, which surveyed the street surrounding the GHQ. The static-filled messages from their shoulder-strapped walkie-talkies meant that they were constantly aware of what was going on. If that wasn't enough, their fingers never left the trigger of their gleaming rifles, which stood out against the olive-green uniforms. There was no doubt these men were trained to kill, and be killed, at a moment's notice.

They had to be on the watch and be ruthlessly professional, not only because they were guarding the sanctum sanctorum of Pakistan's most revered institution, but also because of the threat perception. In October 2009, ten Tehrik-i-Taliban gunmen dressed in military uniform attacked the GHQ, killing nine soldiers and two civilians, and infiltrated the complex, holding many more hostage. The attack was believed to be a response to the Pakistan Army's operations in South Waziristan, its troubled eastern region. They were eventually neutralized by the Pakistan Army's Special Service Group division. Incidentally, the attackers had targeted the same gate we had just entered from. The 2009 attack was a major and unprecedented security breach and sent chills down the spines of the Pakistan Army's top brass. The security of the garrison town in general and the GHQ in particular has been enhanced since.

The Pakistan Army's logo shone bright and proud right in the middle of the gate, displaying two crossed swords, the crescent and star, in bottle green. The entrance, the guards, the buildings inside and the general feel of the place conveyed a sense of imperiousness, professionalism and power, perhaps indicating the place GHQ enjoyed in the Pakistani sociopolitical imagination. The Pakistan Army has always enjoyed pride of place in the minds of the Pakistani civilians. The tall gate and the ruthless guards guarded the men who practically run South Asia's revisionist nuclear-weapon state.

There was complete silence inside the car for some strange reason. Nobody, including the colonel, said a word. It was as if we had instinctively decided to take the Pathan guard's order of not getting out of the car one step further. There wasn't much activity near the gate nor on the path lined with tall street lamps that lay behind the imposing gate. The campus looked quiet too. The Pathan guard seemed to walk around with a curfew-inducing halo around him. That's true power—when you can get someone to do something without even demanding it, all on the strength of your persona.

The guard ended the call and returned to our vehicle, stood still, looked at me once again and asked for my passport, which I had kept ready by then. I handed him my passport with a certain amount of trepidation—there was a reason for it, of course. He held it up to compare my face with the photo on the profile page, and then leafed through to my Pakistan visa. Since I had stapled several pages together, I offered to help him find the visa. He didn't even bother ignoring my offer. I was nervous because the bold letters on the side of the visa read 'not valid for restricted/prohibited area'. There can be no area more prohibited for an Indian than the GHQ in Rawalpindi. My worry stemmed from the memory of my previous year's experience at the gate of the Lahore cantonment, where I was stopped by the 'boys on the motorbike' for violating visa rules. I didn't want to go back from the gate, not after having come this far, driving down all the way from Rawalakot. Not after coming this close to the GHQ.

My 'illegal' entry into the GHQ didn't seem to bother him. Technically, I was already in the prohibited zone, the Rawalpindi garrison. He compared my passport with details on a paper he had with him, returned it and told the colonel that someone would come out to get us soon. He repeated his order—'Do not step out of the vehicle.'

We must have sat inside the car for around five to six minutes. An army vehicle drove down from inside the GHQ and stopped beside us. A young major in smart civvies emerged from the vehicle. This time the Pathan guard was warmer in his salute and stomped his feet on the ground with more vigour. The Pathan and the other men around him saluted the major in unison. The major acknowledged them by raising his right hand, walked up to our car and saluted the colonel. They smiled and chatted briefly. Suddenly, the tension seemed to disappear with the arrival of a gracious major. Even the sniffer dog wagged his tail.

He shook my hands firmly and said, 'Welcome to the GHQ, Professor Jacob. Hope you had a good drive from Rawalakot this morning?' He apologized for making us wait and asked us to follow his car. Curiously, I was not asked to get down from the car for a scan, nor were my bags checked. There was no pre-installed scanner on the gate either. This did take me by surprise: how could an Indian citizen be allowed to enter the seat of power of the Pakistan Army without being put through a thorough scan?

I asked the colonel, not that I expected an answer from him. 'There is no need,' he said with a smile. The smile gave it away. Clearly, they knew 'all about me', but more so, I had been with them for the past three days. They seemed to have checked me out completely.

The Call from Rawalpindi

The afternoon sun knows no borders. It will lull you to sleep, irrespective of which side you're on. The colonel, sitting beside me in the back seat, was pulled out of his afternoon slumber by his ringing phone. The armed men, seated behind us, were half asleep too, their weapons on the floor of the vehicle. The ideal time for an enemy ambush, I thought. The heavy lunch had brought on this afternoon lethargy. The driver tried to find the perfect radio station. The colonel didn't care much for radio music, but he let the driver find the right frequency. After all, he needed him to stay alert as he manoeuvred the vehicle across treacherous roads, hairpin turns and narrow stretches astride steep cliffs. I tried not to look down as the vehicle passed over hairline roads that made gravity seem like fiction.

The Pakistan Army battalion posted at the Tatrinote trading point had offered us a sumptuous meal with locally sourced fresh vegetables and fried river fish caught from the river flowing a stone's throw away. The hospitality was once again remarkable. I had gone to wash up before the meal and had no hint that the brigadier and the officers below him would continue to stand and would not begin their lunch till I took the first plate. I was shocked and humbled—why would they do that? Hospitality in army messes, in India or Pakistan, never fails to amaze, sometimes even embarrass, me.

'Yes, sir, of course, sir, we will be there, sir.' The colonel's conversation on the phone was brief, cryptic and deferential. He turned to me with a smile on his still-sleepy face to deliver the good news. My visit to the GHQ had been cleared at the highest levels of the Pakistan Army, he informed me, and paused as if trying to gauge my reaction. The earlier plan was to meet his bosses at the ISPR, the media wing of the Pakistan Armed

Forces. For some reason, the ISPR top brass wasn't able to meet me, and the colonel was a bit unhappy about it through the afternoon. But eventually he managed to get me an audience with someone higher up than the ISPR generals—the chief of general staff himself, the second most powerful man in the Pakistan Army. I had no complaints. I was thrilled, actually.

'Is Sunday a working day for the GHQ?' I asked the colonel. He confirmed that it wasn't. But, the CGS was apparently making a special appearance for me on a Sunday. Waheed Arshad must have put in a strong recommendation to his junior officer, I assumed, as there was no other reason for the CGS to come in on a non-working Sunday to have lunch with an Indian academic in his office.

Talking to a senior-level officer was important for my work on the LoC and CFVs. Senior officers almost always provide a strategic big-picture view of things, unlike the junior officers on the field who either do not have a bird's-eye view or are constantly looking over their shoulders when sharing it with you. When working on military matters, it helps to start at the top.

There was another reason why I was excited about the lunch. I was, most likely, going to be the first Indian to enter the heart of the GHQ, the office of the CGS, a few metres from the office of General Bajwa, the army chief, himself.

Upon my return to India, I asked journalist Nirupama Subramanian of the *Indian Express* if she had ever visited the GHQ. Nirupama has been a long-time track-II friend ever since she returned from her assignment in Pakistan. A clear-headed analyst with an incisive understanding of all things Pakistan, Nirupama was *The Hindu*'s correspondent in Pakistan from May 2006 to February 2010, winning two prestigious awards in Indian journalism for her coverage from the other side.

'You spent four years in Pakistan, have you been to the GHQ? To the offices of the CGS or the army chief,' I asked Nirupama via text message. She had not. 'When I was there, I was invited to the Strategic Plans Division [SPD], the sanctum sanctorum of Pak nuclear prowess, for a press conference which was held to allay global fears that the crown jewels were about to fall into terrorist hands. 2008. We were some 20–25 foreign journals, and we were taken by bus from the Info dept. I have also been to Army House during Musharraf's time when he had a press conference there. 2006. And I met the Lt. Gen who was heading ISPR in 2006 in his office in Pindi,' she wrote back.[1] So that's the closest an Indian is likely to have been to the GHQ—to the ISPR chief's office and the briefing room of the SPD, as a part of a group. Retired Pakistani army officers confirm that this is the closest to the GHQ that any Indian has come, in their recollection, given that Indian citizens are typically kept out of the GHQ.

The private lunch with the CGS in his office was bound to be different and unprecedented.

The call from Rawalpindi brightened up our afternoon: the lazy slumber was gone, the soldiers picked up their guns off the floor, the driver settled on an FM station playing some faint Sufi music, and the colonel began to give me a brief history of the Rawalpindi city.

We rushed back from Tatrinote. It was important to get to the Rawalakot army mess before dark. Travelling along the LoC at night can be dangerous. You could be a sitting duck. I remember making the journey from Jammu city to the far-flung Billawar district, where I used to be a primary school teacher in 1998, through Samba and Kathua in the 1990s. The only thing worse than the report of machine-gun fire is its echo that reverberates off the surrounding hills, adding a deathly tone to the already sinister soundscape. At night, especially when CFVs were at a high, we would be instructed by the army check posts to turn off the lights of the vehicle. Lights, at home or on the vehicle, would definitely attract firing by the Pakistani side, who would otherwise be firing in the dark. On some occasions we waited till late into the night for the firing to stop and the soldiers to give us the go-ahead to continue our progress towards Billawar, with dimmed lights and bated breath.

The situation was similar as we made our way to Rawalakot, except we were concerned about Indian firing.

There was another reason why we rushed back to the army mess. We had to begin the next day's journey early in the morning. It would take around six hours from Rawalakot to Rawalpindi and the rest depended on the traffic. It was important to catch some sleep before we set out the following day.

We set out at 7 a.m. sharp. The colonel kept Rawalpindi informed of our location and distance from the GHQ so as to coordinate the general's arrival at the GHQ. Music from some distant FM station kept playing in fits and starts. The driver continued to keep fiddling with the radio, mostly in vain.

The road was smooth even though there was some Sunday rush of Pakistanis travelling to Murree for some winter fun. Cars with families and happy children. The latter would often wave at us, as kids everywhere tend to do. In certain places, the roads were clogged due to mudslides. We stopped at a dhaba by the road for some much-needed tea and biscuits. We sat on chairs by the roadside so as to enjoy the crisp morning sun. The colonel was in his best uniform—he was, after all, taking me to the GHQ. The boys at the dhaba and the passers-by smiled at the colonel in respect—the perks of being an army officer in Pakistan.

We sat by the side of the six-lane road, staring at the imposing snow-clad mountaintops on the one hand and the deadly valleys on the other. It was to be my last day on these roads. I may never come back here, I realized. The colonel and I (along with the major and armed men who I never spoke to) had spent a few days together in the most inhospitable, yet breathtakingly beautiful, of terrains. I would soon bid goodbye to them as well. The final glimpse of the steep ranges and valleys suddenly brought a rush of melancholy. There was a strange desire to cling on to that place for a few more minutes before we left the dhaba, as if I had some deep emotional connection with it.

Inside the GHQ

In 1947, when Pakistan became a state independent of British India, the GHQ of the Pakistan Army was established within the premises of the northern command HQ of the British Indian Army. British India had been divided, so had been the militaries and the military assets, with the lion's share going to newly independent India. Even though political power had been handed over to the Pakistani leadership, the Pakistan Army continued to be commanded by General Sir Frank Walter Messervy, a British officer. In India, the Indian Army's British commander in chief was General Sir Roy Bucher. Both Messervy and Bucher were commanded by Field Marshal Sir Claude Auchinleck, the then supreme commander of the Indian and Pakistani defence forces. This was clearly an interesting phase for the two newly independent countries who within months of becoming independent started a war over Kashmir even as their armies were commanded by British generals, both of whom reported to another British general who did not report to the leaderships in India or Pakistan. No wonder then that the war didn't get anywhere, and the dispute continues to this day. In typical colonist fashion, the British took what they could and are nowhere on the scene today. The world has moved on, but the Kashmir question seems to have been frozen in time, only becoming more and more protracted and intermingled with nationalist egos and postcolonial angst.

India and Pakistan became independent in 1947, but the Indian and Pakistani armies have traditions, culture and basic standard operating procedures that go back far beyond 1947, and many of those remain just the same to this day. The two sides understand each other well, and yet they have over the years developed very divergent world views. The Pakistan Army rules the country for most practical purposes, and the Indian Army struggles to have a say in the scheme of things in India. And yet, take a closer comparative look at the two armies and it will surprise you how similar they are. Armies are conservative organizations that don't give up their traditions easily.

The GHQ is within the Rawalpindi garrison complex. There is nothing extraordinary about Rawalpindi, an old run-down city adjacent to the rather new and modern city of Islamabad, Pakistan's flashy capital. Locals refer to it as Pindi, a coinage that's gaining currency in India as well.

The GHQ has a special place in Pakistan, just as Aabpara, the ISI HQ, does. Aabpara may have its own world view and attendant machinations, but at the end of the day it is subsumed within the larger strategic rationale of the GHQ, whose say in matters of national security and strategic vision is indispensable in the Pakistani scheme of things. The GHQ also looms large in the Indian strategic imagination—it is regularly invoked in India to mean the locus of Pakistani strategic decision-making, as the entity that torpedoes the Pakistani civilian government's peace moves with India, as the house of the terror ringmasters of South Asia, and as India's perennial enemy. The GHQ, to the Indian mind, is at the centre of everything that is wrong with Indo-Pak relations;

and I had just entered its heavily guarded complex, driven in an army vehicle with faceless Pakistani soldiers.

We had passed through the giant gate, but the well-secured GHQ complex had several more layers of security, with automatic roadblocks and spike barriers. We would slow down at each layer and the guard would let us pass after he spoke to someone on the phone, and the major in the vehicle in front of us would get a stiff salute. His senior, the colonel in my car, would be ignored. They seemed quite clannish. Well-manicured green spaces, well-maintained buildings, wide roads—there was a look of orderliness and pomp to the place.

The major took us to an office adjacent to that of the CGS in a complex where each office looked like an independent bungalow. The major's subordinates offered us refreshments once we entered the building. In typical army fashion, the major seemed to be prepping me for the meeting with the CGS, chatting me up and indirectly giving me guidance on the impending meeting.

We would walk around 200 metres to get to the office, and it would happen exactly at the same time as the general would step out of his car, he explained. He would go inside his office and I would be received at the door by his deputy who would talk to me for a few seconds and take me inside the room where the CGS would meet me. There would be lunch, following which the general would take his leave of me. Soon thereafter the major would meet me outside General Akbar's office to take me back. I was to carry no phones or cameras; I would be allowed to carry my notebook and pen though. It was to be a minute-to-minute schedule, leaving nothing to chance.

'Any questions?'

'Sounds good,' I responded with a smile.

We were to wait for half an hour for the arrival of Lieutenant General Bilal Akbar and his deputy, the vice

chief of the general staff, Major General Shaheen Mazhar
Mehmood. The residence of the CGS is a few kilometres
away from the GHQ, but a warm winter Sunday is also good
for golf. He might not be too pleased to meet me, I reasoned.

I always imagined the top generals of the Pakistan Army
as belonging to some kind of exclusive society—bound by
oath, blood and honour, and mired in secrecy. The power
they wield is legendary. The formidable corps commanders
and their regular corps commanders' meetings could send
shivers down the spines of the Pakistani political class: 'What
are they up to?' the political class must worriedly wonder,
I imagined. 'That's not quite right.' Tariq Ghazi once told
me, 'It's like any other organization with its own differences,
internal politics, people trying to get ahead of each other. But
once a decision is taken, we carry out those decisions in a
professional manner.'

Sometime in 2003, an Indian politician, R.K. Mishra,
remarked half-jokingly in a closed-door discussion at the
New Delhi–based Observer Research Foundation, which he
headed at the time: 'How many corps commanders are there
in Pakistan? What if we open Swiss bank accounts in their
names and deposit 100 crores in each of those accounts? Will
the Pakistan Army change its policy towards India?' That
was a smart question though everyone who sat around him
laughed. The problem with 'secret societies' and bonds of
brotherhoods is that money may not persuade them. Man,
after all, does not live by bread alone. Power can be equally,
if not more, intoxicating.

'I Was Expecting to Meet an Older Professor'

'Let's head out, the general is here.' The major gestured us
to start walking towards the office of Lieutenant General

Bilal Akbar. While we were walking towards the bungalow housing the general's office, his official vehicle, a black-coloured bulletproof SUV, sped past us, just as the major had briefed me. The timing was perfect, and I was thoroughly impressed. I was curious to see if everything else would go as per the major's plan.

The red-flag-bearing pilot cars and vehicles with jammers were already outside his office, waiting by the side with their engines humming and lights flashing. Armed men with their fingers on the trigger and impersonal looks stood around looking for anything unusual. There were hardly any people beyond the bungalow I was walking towards. Someone ran up to the back door of the car, opened it and stood still. A stout man—that's all I could get from a fleeting glance—stepped out of the car and hurriedly stepped into the building. The guards stiffened and saluted him, which he customarily ignored. The door closed behind him, but the milieu continued to be formal for several more minutes.

I made it a point to walk behind the colonel and the major—why take chances? The stiff guards were yet to ease up when I reached the front door. While I was being ushered into the building they continued to be 'in attention'—they didn't know I was an Indian civilian. I smiled at the guard who opened the door and asked customarily in Hindi/Urdu, 'How are you?' It was a habit I had developed lately, something I observed tended to break the ice and make people warmer. Not this time—the tall, young guard merely said 'assalamualaikum'. Formality is impersonal, I was learning quickly. In any case, I had learnt to respond to 'assalamualaikum' by then, in the correct Islamic manner.

I took a deep breath as I walked into the office of General Akbar. Known to be a no-nonsense officer, his reputation preceded him. He had taken over from Lieutenant General

Rizwan Akhtar as the CGS of the Pakistan Army exactly a year ago. He was previously the director general of the Pakistan Rangers, Karachi, a paramilitary force almost entirely officered by the Pakistan Army. As DG Rangers, he was reputed to have 'cleaned up the city' by going after the troublemakers. But then there were also allegations of human rights violations against him, which his forces had allegedly committed while 'cleaning up the city'. General Akbar had a reputation in Pakistan; whether it was positive or negative depended on who one talked to.

The CGS is uniquely placed in the Pakistan Army, and wields a great deal of power. The Pakistan Army chief commands the army, but the CGS runs it—so they say in the army circles. While the chief is selected by the prime minister, the selection of the CGS is entirely the chief's prerogative, which he does also on the basis of who among the lieutenant generals of the army he has an excellent chemistry with. Bilal Akbar was one of the junior lieutenant generals of the army when he was selected as Bajwa's CGS. Waheed Arshad was also the junior-most lieutenant general when Chief Kayani made him CGS. Being junior, however, is hardly seen as an impediment to being able to carry out the tough tasks of the CGS, Arshad recalled to me once.

The CGS and his office form the fulcrum of the Pakistan Army's diverse engagements, and as it is well known, the Pakistan Army has traditionally had more responsibilities and power than other armies. The laundry list of his day-to-day responsibilities includes army operations, dealing with intelligence issues, focusing on the development of the arsenal, and dealing with defence budget–related issues and manpower aspects. The CGS also interfaces with the International Security Assistance Force (ISAF) in Afghanistan as well as with the civilian establishment based in Islamabad on most matters of security, disaster management, foreign policy issues and internal security, among others. In short, the CGS occupies the hot seat in the GHQ. He has a secretariat to manage this wide range of responsibilities, with two vice chiefs of general staff (both major generals, assigned an army major each as staff officers) to assist him in his duties. The secretariat of the CGS is headed by a lieutenant colonel, with two majors working under him.

So how does the Pakistan Army function as the country's power centre? Unlike what many people think, Pakistani generals tell me, the Pakistan Army does not bulldoze its way to dictating terms to the civilian/political establishment in Islamabad, but rather uses a slew of methods including negotiations, reasoned analysis, etc., to push its agenda with Islamabad. They prepare policy papers and present them to the various arms of the civilian government, participate in various official meetings and give their views, and call on various officials to suggest measures on defence and security issues. It's done subtly, they insist.

There is a reason why the chemistry between the chief and his CGS is important: the army chief and the CGS work in close coordination, with the latter carrying out the policy decisions of the former. They meet almost on a daily basis and, as is the case with the rest of the GHQ, are constantly in touch with each other via secure systems online and secure telephone connections.

The chief General Bajwa's office is hardly 25 metres from the office of the CGS. Put differently, power in Pakistan flowed from 25 metres from where I was standing.

'Welcome to GHQ, Jacob.' Major General Shaheen Mazhar Mehmood received me as soon as I walked into the room. Mehmood is an easy smiler with a warm personality. He shook hands with me and went on to hug the young major.

Given how his seniors and others treated him, I got the feeling that he was a rising star who was expected to do well in the years to come.

Mehmood was earlier the inspector general of the Frontier Corps based in Peshawar in Pakistan's KP province. 'Come on in, the CGS will see you in a minute,' he said. All of this happened in such a hurry and in quick succession that I failed to register his name and designation. In any case, none of them were wearing their army uniforms. It was only much later during the lunch that I realized that he was the deputy CGS.

We entered the CGS's office through the main door, which led to a room with a huge table. On one side was a seating area and on the other side was the dining area. There were several doors which housed the offices of his deputies and officers. It looked like a living apartment—but it was not. In the main hall, to the left, there was a large table which looked like the CGS's workstation. There were crossed swords on the wall and miniature weapon systems placed on the table. The office looked magisterial, imperial and awe-inspiring.

On the right-hand side of the room, there was a small table which could be used as a meeting table or a dining table. There were a few waiters standing around with trays of coloured drinks. There were a few adjacent rooms from where the uniformed waiters emerged with their trays and headgear.

A side door opened and a short, bespectacled and moustached man in his mid-fifties emerged. He was also in casual civilian clothes and was wearing a bright T-shirt, dark pants and a pair of white sports shoes—it looked as if he had reluctantly pulled himself away from the golf course that Sunday morning. Everything around him seemed to stiffen up suddenly, all over again—the major general, the young major, the waiters. Someone had to break the silence.

General Akbar looked at me intently for a few seconds before uttering, 'Welcome to Pakistan, and the GHQ.' He bears a strong-willed handshake and a miserly smile, and speaks thoughtfully. 'Hope you had a good trip to the LoC.' The awkwardness in the air was still refusing to go away. 'I must confess,' he said after a few more awkward seconds, 'I was expecting to meet an older professor from India.'

'I will come again after a few years when I am older, general saab,' I responded with a smile. He laughed loudly, as did his deputy and the young major, though not the waiters. Some of the awkwardness helpfully vanished. We got down to business.

'I have read your work, but you don't seem to give much importance to the political factors behind ceasefire violations. Since the arrival of the Modi government in New Delhi, CFVs are mostly caused by political triggers. Modi wants to show that he is a strong prime minister and hence the violence on the LoC. Rest assured, we will retaliate as and when we are fired at,' he said, beginning the conversation on an accusatory note. I wasn't too keen on getting into an argument with him, so I focused on my favourite thesis about tactical factors causing CFVs and he agreed that in the absence of political triggers, tactical causes become predominant. That even the serving generals in Rawalpindi agreed with my thesis both delighted and relieved me.

'What about the question of terror? Is that not the most significant issue between India and Pakistan, including causing CFVs?' I asked him. He stressed two aspects relating to terrorism: one, how the Pakistan Army has been able to defeat terrorism in FATA and two, how what happens in Kashmir is spontaneous and locally driven. 'We only give diplomatic support,' he told me, sticking to the Pakistan Army's official line on the matter. I didn't want to be pushing my line beyond a point. I was not meeting the CGS to confirm what I already knew, but to get a sense of things, to read between the lines and, most importantly, to be physically present at the GHQ. I wasn't there for a scoop. It was more of an intellectual pilgrimage.

Leaning towards the table, with his elbows on the edge, General Akbar spoke fast, without a break, and tended to avoid eye contact. He seemed as if he was careful about what he was saying even though he didn't have a problem engaging with any and every question or talking at length. His deputy, General Mehmood, was mostly quiet and kept taking notes or answered when General Akbar asked him to pitch in. Mehmood seemed observant and mostly looked at his boss rather than me. I kept my notebook open and religiously jotted down everything that was being said in the room, asked questions and observed the two men sitting before me. For some strange reason, the uneasiness in the room continued to persist despite our best efforts. A place of that kind does that, perhaps.

The lunch arrived soon thereafter: chicken fried rice, mutton curry, vegetables and spiced curd. I avoided the meat and let the waiter serve a portion of rice on to my plate, assuming it was vegetarian. It wasn't. There were pieces of chicken in it. I didn't want to be seen complaining about the dish nor did I want to break the flow of Akbar's long answer. I kept nodding at him and pushing tiny pieces of fried chicken to the side of the plate. The observant Mehmood asked the waiter to serve me vegetable fried rice instead, which was done rather quickly. Akbar kept talking, unmindful of the small mayhem caused by my troubles with fried chicken. The lunch in general was a let-down, but not the conversation with the generals.

Akbar stressed the terrorism question once again—he knew the importance of messaging on terror. 'We have done a great job of flushing out the terrorists from the FATA region. Actually, you must come and visit the place. You should see it for yourself.' Mehmood nodded in agreement.

My heart suddenly leapt in anticipation of a visit to the FATA region, which would be yet another unique experience for me. But did he really mean it? Perhaps he did—Arshad had also mentioned the possibility of such a visit.

'Wow, that's a great job. It would be a great honour to visit FATA, general.'

Since 2001, close to a dozen antiterror operations have been launched by the Pakistan Army in the FATA region, with Operation Zarb-e-Azb, launched in 2014, being the largest of these. According to reports, Pakistan's military operations in FATA have displaced around 2 million people.

'You should. My chief and I are very clear that well-meaning Indian academics and journalists should be welcomed to visit Pakistan and see for themselves the progress we are making on several fronts. On the economic front, we are working with the Chinese on several projects. In fact, by refusing to join the various regional connectivity projects, India is losing out.'

'I am aware of the Pakistan Army's campaigns against terrorism,' I said, 'but why no action against India-centric terror groups?'

'We are dealing with them on the basis of urgency. We are bogged down with one set of antiterror operations. Of course, we will not let any terror outfits to operate from our country. Any terrorist is a threat to us.'

Lunch was over, but we continued to sit around the small corner table as the waiters removed the plates and leftover food. Green tea was brought in and the conversation continued. The lunch meeting was now stretching to its limits.

'I will take your leave now,' Akbar said as he shook my hand. 'I hope to see you again, here in Pakistan. Good luck with your work.'

Mehmood saw me off at the door. 'If you need anything while you are still here, please call me. Take my number from the major.' I had learnt to recognize the significance of pleasantries and not to push their symbolic limits. I neither asked for the number nor was it given to me.

The guards were once again still, the major saluted the general and took charge of me from him. While we walked towards the major's office, General Akbar's cavalcade went past us. Everything had gone as per the major's plans.

In another ten minutes, our car drove past the gate. I looked back for one last glimpse of the Pathan guard who stood still and tall at the gate, uninterested.

6

Among Brothers in Arms

The Statesman

The soft-spoken officer from Military Intelligence (MI), India, was quizzing me: what was I doing in Udhampur, why did I want to meet the northern army commander, and what would I do with my interviews and the impending visit to the LoC in J&K, among other concerns. He jotted down my answers in a pocket-sized notebook and occasionally asked for a few inane clarifications. I was seated in the army commander's office complex, in his staff officer's room. I showed my discomfort by asking him whether he was posted with the GOC's office. Once I realized he was from MI, I answered all his questions diligently, with more details than necessary. In all probability, he already knew why I was there and he might have been detailed to check me out. It's never wise to fool around with the spooks.

The northern army commander's imposing office complex is located on top of a hill in J&K's Udhampur town, in the Jammu division. It commands three crucial corps of the Indian Army—the XIV, XV and XVI corps—deployed in the restive J&K state. I had arrived at the Northern Command HQ an hour ago from the Jammu airport. The commander's staff officer had arranged for me to meet the general as soon as he would arrive. Several onlookers, uniformed and otherwise, in the staff officer's room looked at me as if I was some weird species when I stated, in response to someone's query, that I was there to meet the commander in connection with a book I was writing. 'Write a book? There is a pitched battle going on at the LC [that's how the Indian officers refer to the LoC] and some people are busy writing books'—that's what I imagine their mental reaction must have been.

'I will call you back as soon as I land. I am getting into a chopper,' the commander had told me when I called him a few weeks prior to my arrival in Udhampur. He called back a few hours later and we spoke. 'Come to Udhampur,' he said. 'I will ensure you get a good look at the LC and will try and answer your questions.'

It was June 2016. I had never worked closely with Indian Army officials, except the retired generals whom I had interacted with in the track-II circuits or at an occasional lecture at various staff colleges. I had written several letters to the army HQ in New Delhi exploring the possibility of a visit to the LoC. I took the non-response in my stride as I had in any case not anticipated a positive response. That's when I requested my track-II colleague Lieutenant General Aditya Singh ('Atty' as he is fondly called by his friends in the army) to intervene. Singh is a former southern army commander, and a thoughtful man. He was, while in service, the incumbent northern army commander's senior in the army. Such connections matter more than anything. My trip to the LoC was arranged within the following week. Even though I wasn't too worried about the non-response from the army HQ in New Delhi, I kept wondering why my letters had never been answered.

Staff officers and their offices are intriguing, to say the least. You get to witness things that never happen anywhere else in the army. It is not uncommon to find a young officer, in this case a colonel, surrounded by senior officers who want a word with the army commander/GOC/brigadier, as the case may be. They humour the junior officer, ask about his well-being, and then inquire about the boss's mood, his travel plans, others who have been meeting the boss, etc. The office has a lot of gossip and is the nerve centre of all action that takes place under the boss's area of responsibility. The seniors want gossip, and the staff officer enjoys delivering it.

While I was in the middle of getting quizzed in one corner of the rather spacious room, and eavesdropping on military gossip in another corner, a pilot Gypsy arrived in the parking lot. Several more bulletproof vehicles arrived, and heavily armed soldiers stepped out of the vehicles and took position in the vicinity. Soon thereafter, a tall elderly gentleman emerged from one of the vehicles. The gossip and chit-chat in the staff officer's room suddenly disappeared and a veil of seriousness engulfed it. Everyone in his vicinity either stood in attention or saluted him. Someone who seemed like the senior-most officer shook hands with him. The commander smiled and spoke a few words to those appearing to be his immediate juniors and walked into his office.

Some of the senior officers went to meet him first, and I was in no particular hurry. General Aditya Singh had told me in New Delhi that the army commander was a fine gentleman who would be positive about my work and ensure that I got a ringside view of things. I had come all the way from New Delhi with a lot of expectations and excitement.

Finally, my turn came and I was ushered into the room that was guarded by a tough-looking Gurkha soldier who had a knife with a curved blade attached to his waist. The army commander was commissioned into the Gorkha Rifles in 1976. That explained the Gurkha soldier and his awe-inspiring knife.

As the conversation progressed, I asked the army commander whether my letters to the HQ in New Delhi had reached him. 'No,', he said, paused for a few seconds and laughed. 'In fact, I checked with the HQ when I received your mail about inviting you to the LoC. The advice given to me was that while I could choose to do what I thought was necessary, it might be a good idea to keep away from you.' I was amused—while he had not disobeyed any direct orders from the army HQ in New Delhi, he had decided to overlook their advice. Not everyone would do something like that. It takes a certain kind of man in uniform to do that, someone with a broader view of strategic issues.

I wasn't surprised at what the HQ had told him. The stony silence from the HQ in Delhi had made it clear to me that the men who had scanned my request were not too keen on letting me have a tour of the LoC. As an academic and columnist, I have critiqued several institutions of the Indian state, including the army. 'Why are you so hypercritical of the government and its institutions?' my students at JNU often asked me.

'Because I want them to do better; because we deserve better; because we can do better,' I would respond.

'So what made you decide against the advice of your HQ and invite me here?' I asked the commander; I was curious.

'You will write the book anyway, so I thought it's a good idea to give you my perspective. It's better for me to have my perspective in your book than not having it. And in any case, you are doing what academics should do and I find no problems with it.' His rationale sounded clever and statesmanlike at the same time.

Lieutenant General Deependra Singh Hooda (since retired) is a tall, soft-spoken man with a gentle smile and a strategic view of things. He is a commanding figure who likes to inspire his men rather than impose his will upon them, as his juniors would tell me in the following days. Often enough one finds senior generals with a tactical vision focusing on today and its minute details, generalship failing to change their narrow world view. Hooda is different. He has an excellent appreciation of the big picture, based on which he gave me an understanding of why CFVs occur on the LoC.

His penchant for big-picture analysis didn't prevent him from planning and executing tactical operations. In September 2016, Hooda planed and oversaw the first-ever 'publicized' surgical strikes by the Indian Army, ordered by the then BJP government in power at the Centre. While it was not the first time that the Indian Army (or for that matter, even the Pakistan Army) carried out such operations across the LoC, the fact that this was declared and owned up to made a huge difference. The BJP government in New Delhi milked its political value to the hilt, even while advising others 'not to politicize' national security issues. When the operations were carried out, there were many sceptics in India who questioned the veracity of these operations, just as there were those who argued that the operations failed to achieve the strategic objectives. Hooda's clarification, which he made after retirement—that he could confirm that the videos were real—put an end to the controversy about the authenticity of the operation, if not its strategic utility.

Since retirement, Hooda has become a prominent commentator on strategic issues and regularly writes hard-hitting columns often criticizing the policies of the very government that he took orders from not too long ago. That, to me, shows a man's character.

'I like to retain my ability to say it as I see it,' he told me when I spoke to him over the phone about his thoughtful columns, and whether he would like to join the track-II fraternity where I was keen to get him. 'If I join the track-II efforts, people could potentially cast aspersions on my views . . . not now. I want to say what I want without any handicap.'

It was my day one with the Indian Army in Kashmir and the meeting with the commander had motivated me to continue with my work. The curious man from the MI waited for the meeting to get over so that he could walk me to my car, all the while persisting with his questions, of course. As I sat in my cab, I gave him my visiting card and told him he could call me any time for a clarification about my visit. He never called me. Spooks don't call you, they just drop by when you least expect them.

I was thrilled—perhaps even a wee bit arrogant—at the prospect of going on a visit of the LoC on the recommendation of the army commander, the man whose direct command every Indian soldier and officer on the LoC came under. His writ ran along the entire stretch of the LoC in J&K—and his guest would undoubtedly find the journey smooth and easy, I reasoned.

That overconfident hope survived less than twenty-four hours. I was in for a rude shock.

The Hot-Headed Brigadier

'You are ten minutes late and I don't like anyone turning up late at my office no matter who they are,' the brigadier said, clearly annoyed, looking at me as I was led into his office by a colonel. He seemed angry and ignored my greeting. I apologized to him and looked fleetingly at the colonel to see if he wanted to offer an explanation on why I was ten minutes late for the 10 a.m. meeting. His delay in fetching me from the army mess to take me to the brigadier's office was responsible for the latter's anger. Clearly, there was no way I could have found my way to the brigadier's office inside of an army formation a few kilometres short of the LoC. Wouldn't the brigadier have known that?

At the same time, for an army formation based in a highly sensitive location such as Rajouri, J&K, a ten-minute delay could easily be the difference between life and death—so I did appreciate the brigadier's anger, in retrospect. Sure, discipline matters. But at that moment, I was caught off guard, and didn't really know what to say. Frankly, I hadn't expected such cold behaviour, not after my warm conversation with his boss, the affable General Hooda, the previous evening. The colonel who had accompanied me from the mess stood mum, meek and helpless in front of his senior officer. I noticed fear and embarrassment on his face: fear of the brigadier and embarrassment at having slipped up in the presence of a stranger. I decided not to put him in trouble, and took responsibility for being late. 'My apologies, I can come later if you are busy,' I told the brigadier, who was officiating as the GOC (a post held by an officer at the rank of a major general) of the 25th Infantry Division of the Indian Army, based in Rajouri. The brigadier was on a temporary appointment GOC, and was punching above his weight.

I later asked his junior officers about him: 'Is he always like this?' He is hot-headed, I was told. 'Super efficient, but not easy to work with,' another said. He had a reputation of being a hard taskmaster and unpredictable. Perhaps, I imagined, that was one of the key reasons for him being posted in a critical location like the 25 division HQ in Rajouri, a location that was bombarded by Pakistani shells fairly frequently. You need men like him (and Brigadier Noor of the 2-AK/PoK brigade in PoK whose area of responsibility was not too far from there, on the other side of the LoC) to man treacherous terrains like Rajouri, and Rawalakot. Such people, by their very presence, can either bring about peace and calm in violence-prone areas or cause even more violence. Their fame precedes them. But they can certainly be a pain to deal with.

Certain regiments and officers have a unique reputation. The counterparts on the other side of the sector/area would know about the reputation of the incoming battalion/officer and this could trigger certain dynamics between the two sides. General Panag once told me, 'Each unit has its own reputation which is known to both sides. Within the army, the individual commanders are chosen for the job depending upon the unit's characteristics, its performance and its value systems that are assigned to it.' For instance, he recalled the reputation of the 4th Sikh Regiment when he was part of it and was posted on the LoC: 'In 1968 when my unit, 4 Sikh, went to a sector on the LoC which witnessed sporadic firing, our CO [commanding officer] sent [out] a message that "*Jo ho gaya, so ho gaya, ab 4 Sikh aa gayi hai*" [What's happened has happened, now the 4 Sikh is here], so now if you guys do any mischief you are going to have it.' This had a calming effect in the area.

The 25 division was commanded by such a man, a hot-headed brigadier who wouldn't think twice about launching an operation, or be fussy with his boss's guest. As his juniors put it: '*Yeh aage-peeche nahi dekhta hai* (He is a bold guy).'

The Sikh brigadier with an unfriendly demeanour, deep baritone and a somewhat hostile attitude asked me to be seated and ordered the colonel to leave the room—he did so quickly. I was mentally prepared for another lecture about punctuality and discipline. It was my second day on the LoC, and I decided to give it a few more minutes before staging a walkout and giving a call to the army commander. 'What nonsense!' I thought to myself. I was on the edge of my chair, literally. But I was in for yet another surprise.

'I have been reading all your articles and they are very informative. I have even made a file of your writings which I sent to my son who is preparing for the civil services examination. So you aren't an unknown entity to me.' He smiled.

'Don't take any offence. I just wanted to send a message to the colonel. It's important to keep the boys on their toes,' he said as if he realized that the colonel's time mismanagement had got me late for the meeting.

I sat back and sighed in relief. He ordered green tea with honey and some biscuits.

For the next hour or so, the brigadier gave me a bird's-eye view of the recurrent CFVs in his area. The brigadier was a no-nonsense man who wasn't charitable with the truth. 'Not all violations are initiated by the Pakistani side, unlike what the Indian media would like you to believe,' he said candidly, and more importantly, 'There is hardly any infiltration here so most of the ceasefire violations are a result of strategic and political developments in India and Pakistan.' He also went on to argue that both sides place IEDs in each other's territory to ambush each other's patrol parties, again something one wouldn't hear very frequently.

'Does India have BAT teams to carry out operations inside Pakistan?' I asked him after a moment of hesitation. I was hesitant because the Indian Army has traditionally denied that it has such teams and most officers are reluctant to talk about it.

'Of course we do . . . [They] are constituted for specific operations as and when needed, but they aren't called BATs . . .' He seemed to be in a mood to indulge me. 'Let's be clear, it's a bloody stand-off here, and there are no saints in situations like this,' he went on.

I had already started to like the man when he asked me to get up and come close to his desktop computer, which was placed on a side table. He offered me a chair. 'Take a look. These are clips of our recent operations against the Pakistani posts. We pounded them and razed their posts to the ground,' he said, proudly explaining the calibre of the various weapon systems used in the clips he was showing me on his computer. The black-and-white clips showed firing by heavy weapons and how the targets went up in a cloud of smoke with a deafening noise. Obviously, as a layman I couldn't tell who was firing at whom and when and where. 'Needless to say, you have not seen any of these clips,' he quipped. He went on to explain the weapon systems used, the manner in which such attacks are mounted and how it unsettles the Pakistani side.

By the time the meeting came to an end, the officer had become quite talkative and forthcoming, briefly shedding his reputation for being tough and the initial lack of enthusiasm. 'You know, there is only so much I can tell and show since you are here via official channels. Come again in your private capacity and I will take you to places you will never go to and show you things that you won't believe existed,' he said with a serious look after he asked his men to fetch the colonel. I looked at him curiously. Perhaps he realized I wasn't totally convinced by his rather out-of-the-box offer, so he continued, 'I mean it. I will send my own vehicle to the airport to pick you up if you decide to come.'

My next stop was a hotspot called the Bhimber Gali brigade, and I thought about the brigadier's offer throughout the bumpy ride to our destination. For the academic in me, the brigadier's invitation was exceptionally appealing. I have always believed that if academics have to be noticed, they need to have insights into the system and should be able to observe the system from within. This then was that opportunity. Perhaps I should have returned to Rajouri for the forbidden rendezvous with the hot-headed brigadier.

And yet, there was something in me that prevented me from accepting that offer. I returned to New Delhi a few days later but didn't take up the offer. I let it pass—and I was pleased about doing so. I felt I would be crossing my self-imposed redline if I were to take up that offer, especially since it might fall in the grey zone for an academic and I simply didn't want to be in that zone. Besides the 'grey zone' worry, I was also concerned because I was trying to go to the Pakistani side of the LoC and so I wanted everything I did on the Indian side to be above board and, as they say in the official circles, 'through proper channels'.

Several weeks after I returned to JNU, the brigadier rang me up to say that he had seen an article I wrote about my journey on the LoC and IB in *The Hindu*.[1] He said he was in agreement with everything I had written, except how I had unwittingly equated the work of the army and that of the BSF: 'Please don't compare us to the BSF. That is a central police organization.' I didn't insist that it was a paramilitary organization. Perhaps his hot-headedness had made me a bit wary. 'See, I keep a watch on you,' he said before hanging up, and we both laughed.

Life in a Bunker

'That is a Pakistani post.' The colonel pointed at a bunker around 100 metres down the slope. The bunker had a high-flying Pakistani flag, a few peepholes and was heavily barricaded with what looked like a stone wall. There was thick foliage around the bunker and tall trees bent over it, as if trying to protect it. Almost nothing else about the bunker was visible from the spot we were at, inside an Indian bunker perched on top of a hill.

'Do you want to take a closer look at it?' one of the Indian soldiers asked me, handing me his binoculars. The Pakistani flag was more visible now; what looked like some clothes were hanging out to dry. 'During last month's CFVs we shot down their flag,' said the soldier with pride. The childlike enthusiasm of the soldier as he delightedly described how the Pakistani flag was brought to the ground was unmissable.

He was a part of the Hamirpur battalion, commanded by one Colonel Chatterjee. Chatterjee had taken me to the MST post, which offers a good view of one of Pakistan's more vulnerable posts. This was an area where Indians had complete domination. Earlier in the day, I had arrived at the Bhimber Gali brigade HQ, one of those areas which frequently report cross-border firing. After a courtesy call to the brigadier, we set out to visit Indian posts. The Bhimber area which lay south of the Pir Panjal region had a somewhat warm daytime temperature in June, unlike the Kashmir region, which lay north of the mountain range.

What I loved the most was visiting the posts and bunkers of the Indian Army on the LoC. In fact, I was excited about it and there was a reason behind my excitement. An army post or post-cum-bunker is the first line of defence on the LoC, and it houses alert and armed soldiers, arms and ammunition. The heavily barricaded posts have sleeping barracks, colourful pictures of gods and goddesses, and the personal items of men, including the photographs of their loved ones. Such posts can usually sustain themselves for at least a week, which becomes important during prolonged periods of cross-border firing. Amidst such tension, not much outside assistance might come to them but, more importantly, the inhabitants of those basic habitats might not even be able to step out—show your head and you might get shot at.

During such periods, a soldier's life is replete with monotony and fear. When he is not on active duty, which is barely a few hours, he is busy observing the opponent's post through binoculars or telescopic guns. He is free to take aim and shoot if he sees a soldier within the range of his gun. Similarly, he could be shot at by the other side. Life is cheap there.

Indian officers talk about sniper attacks by Pakistani soldiers or Rangers or even terrorists. In fact, there have been several media reports of sniping incidents both on the LoC and IB in J&K. Rakesh Sharma of the BSF once told me that sniping takes a serious toll on a soldier's morale: 'A man standing on duty at the post is always under tremendous fear of being watched by the opposite side through a telescopic rifle and of being shot at any moment.'

Notwithstanding the fear of death and extreme boredom, which they seem to have learnt to accept over the years, they made the best chai and pakoras in those posts. Some of them had perfected the art of making chai and pakoras to such an extent that sometimes senior officers paid visits to certain posts, on hearing about the tasty snacks prepared there. In fact, men at every post I went to ensured that they served me those wonderful snacks, perhaps appreciating the difficult journey that I often had to undertake to reach them.

Many of these far-flung posts have nothing that even remotely resembles a road connection, and getting there can be quite a challenge unless you are prepared for a long trek. Animals, mostly donkeys, are typically used to ferry loads into those remote posts. In some cases, they also rear livestock near the post so as to procure animal products for subsistence. That men serving on the front lines strive to make a home out of such inhospitable environments is a triumph of the human spirit. Ahead of the living quarters, there is usually a fortified bunker from where enemy movements can be observed. The living quarters do not normally face the adversary for obvious reasons, and wherever possible they are located on the reverse slope, hidden away from the adversary's gaze.

A casual visitor to the posts might wonder why there is no rhyme or reason behind the location of these posts. They were not erected based on a predetermined plan. Even the LoC wasn't a result of prior mutually-agreed-upon plans. The Kashmir border, historically speaking, is the result of the first India–Pakistan war over Kashmir in 1947–48. The location of troops in 1947 became the Cease-Fire Line, which became the LoC in 1972. Between 1948 and 1972, not much of the line changed although the nomenclature did.

What is even more interesting to note is that there is often a lack of clarity regarding the line. In other words, the LoC is a notional line and not a real one. The LoC has only been delineated on a map and not demarcated on the ground. Translating what's on the map to how it should be on the ground has posed major differences and stand-offs.

Retired Indian brigadier Gurmeet Kanwal explained to me that while in strongly held areas like Tangdhar the LoC is well-understood, in lightly held areas such as Gurez and Machil, it is more of a perception. 'So when I construct a bunker where I think my territory lies, the Pakistani guy fires because he says it is on their side,' he said. Weather, torrential rains, snowfall and soil erosion, etc., can also cause a lack of clarity on the LoC. When asked, a serving Indian general in Kupwara told me categorically that 'on the ground, the LoC is an assumed line'.

The lack of clarity not only leads to an occasional jostle for territory but even to the inadvertent crossing of civilians and soldiers to the other side. In September 2016, it was reported that an Indian soldier, Chandu Chavan, 'inadvertently crossed over' from his post in the Mendhar sector of the LoC. In February 2013, Pakistan reported a similar incident of a Pakistani soldier crossing over to the Indian side in the Khuiratta sector.

On our way to the Behroti village, I was keen on visiting a post perched on top of a lush green mountain, overlooking several Pakistani posts and Indian and Pakistani villages, and way beyond the Indian fence. The colonel tried to dissuade me, given the steep climb and extreme exposure to the Pakistani side. I persisted with my request and finally we walked up the inhospitable 2-kilometre stretch to reach a secluded army post surrounded by trees and bushes.

We were received by several armed men who were looking down upon us during our climb as if to provide cover. A handsome young man carrying an AK-47 emerged from the post and saluted the colonel. The young captain had just arrived on the LoC after his training. With a BTech degree from IIT Delhi, and excellent job prospects in the private sector, the captain was braving Pakistani bullets in an isolated Indian Army post at least a kilometre beyond the Indian fence. It would not be an exaggeration to say that during tense border stand-offs, he and his men would be sitting ducks. I wondered why he had chosen this life. 'It's the love for the uniform. I just couldn't get rid of this childhood dream of donning the army uniform. Money is unimportant,' he said. He spoke very little and in monosyllables when he did. Perhaps the presence of a colonel deterred him, or he was still getting used to the utter shock of being on the LoC. We chatted about the two neighbouring campuses, IIT and JNU, and the neighbouring markets and the local dhabas, about heroism, valour and living and dying for the motherland. Talking to the young captain that afternoon was a humbling experience. Here was a highly educated and cultured young man with huge monetary prospects sharing a bunker, meals and jokes with men who had nothing to boast of in terms of education, though most of them were senior to him in age and experience. As we chatted on, I realized that we came from completely different worlds, held hugely divergent world views, did different things in life, and yet there was something that connected us: Was it our common humanity or cosmic civilizational Indianness? I couldn't quite articulate it.

The Nowhere People

Identity and sovereignty take on completely different meanings in an area where borders are blurred and political lines on a map don't correspond to actual geographical/residential divides. What India means in New Delhi is poles apart from what it means to a person living 100 metres from Pakistan. His/her relatives are on either side of the LoC. They can see each other from across the border but they can never meet. Here, the Indian state is present through the barrel of a gun. On the LoC, nationalism often feels oppressive and existential questions are all too real.

Nationalism is what we make of it—the idea of nationalism differs from one interpreter to another. In postnational Europe it has different meanings which differ from what we have in South Asia. I have travelled seamlessly within the European Union, across nations, without being stopped, once even travelling from Germany to France by air without being asked for an id proof—even though this is where the idea of nation was born and nurtured and in whose name countless wars were waged, and millions of civilians were killed. Today, those borders have opened up and one would find many people travelling from one country to another for work on a daily basis. Nationalism doesn't define their humanity or destiny any more.

Life in Behroti village in the Mendhar tehsil of the Poonch district symbolizes the worst that modern states and nationalism can do to people. What's even worse is that they won't talk about it, or rather, they would tell you the exact opposite of what they feel, more often than not. That's what nationalism does to you—it makes you do and say things you wouldn't otherwise. People like us don't realize the inherent double-talk, but the ones physically inhabiting the fringes of the territorial state do.

Behroti village lies about a kilometre ahead of the Indian fence on the LoC. While the border fence doesn't officially signify the end of Indian sovereignty, for most practical purposes this is where the social contract between the state and its citizens becomes shaky. Residents of the village have to strictly abide by specific timings to 'enter India' through one of the gates in the fence (guarded by the Indian Army troops) and get their identity cards checked. A hundred metres ahead of their village is a Pakistani village where their estranged relatives live. While in India, a fence separates them from their compatriots, but there is no fence between them and their relatives in Pakistan, both of whom live under the prying gaze of the Indian and Pakistani soldiers. For them, there are effectively three entities: Pakistan on one side, India on the other, and themselves, caught in the middle. Living in the village is like walking on broken glass every time you step out of your house.

Do they sometimes go back and forth? They say 'never', and so do the Indian soldiers. But then both of them have a reason to say so. There are stories about cross-border love affairs and villagers risking bullets in the dead of night during relatively peaceful times to visit their relatives on the other side. Pakistani forces do not normally object; Indian forces do. But risk-taking is a part of human nature. More so, asking poor villagers to go to New Delhi to get a Pakistan visa and then travel to Lahore, then to Islamabad and then to PoK and finally to the village to meet one's close relative who lives 500 metres away from their home is tragic. One young man narrated the story of precisely such a visit he undertook some years ago to meet his ailing grandmother on the other side. 'Didn't you try crossing over at night?' I asked. He merely smiled.

Such informal interactions were far more frequent before the 1980s, but they have certainly not stopped. Some estimate that in the Bhimber Gali area, 40 per cent of those living ahead of the fence, close to the zero line, have relatives living on the other side.

These people are Indians today, but until 1971, they were Pakistanis. Unlike after the 1965 war, India and Pakistan did not exchange territories that were captured during the 1971 war in J&K, even though in other states such exchanges of captured territories took place. So Behroti was captured by the Indian forces and by the time the war came to an end, the erstwhile village was cut in half, with families getting divided right in the middle. Now imagine this happening overnight and having to relive that experience for decades thereafter to this day.

Behroti's citizens have been both Indians and Pakistanis, and have Pakistani relatives. Does their situation often spring a certain angst in them about the self and nationhood? I wondered. Colonel Ravinder Gahlawat, the man who took me there, did tell me—much later when I met him in New Delhi—that when their spirit is down, they often come up and ask: 'Whose people are we?' Especially when the civilian administration refuses to give them the benefits of statehood, or when an aggressive soldier talks rudely to them, or when they have to stay indoors due to crossfire. The place has seen little development since 1972, thanks to recurrent firing and tension, and the civilian officials have been unwilling to risk their lives to carry out developmental activities there. During the Kargil War the entire village had to be vacated.

In 2015, Colonel Ravinder Gahlawat stepped in to help make them feel more at 'home'. The colonel and his brigadier—H.S. Sahi of the Bhimber Gali brigade—started out by completing a road project which had been stuck since 1971.

Behroti is not the only village ahead of the fence. There are several villages like this which got stranded ahead of the Indian fence in the 2001–03 period. Pakistan does not have a border fence and so technically there are no villages ahead of the fence even though there are villages close to the zero line. In the Tithwal area of Kashmir, which I once visited on a day-long trip, there are thirteen villages, located ahead of the fence.

In the Jammu division alone (including Kathua, Samba, Jammu, Rajouri and Poonch), there are around 590 villages at a distance between 0 and 5 kilometres from the IB/LoC, of which 448 villages are vulnerable due to CFVs, according to the Indian Ministry of Home Affairs.[2]

Major violations result in the mass displacement of people from their land. In 2014, for instance, 73,368 persons from Jammu, Kathua and Samba were displaced due to CFVs. While it is common for villagers to live in their homes ahead of the fence along the LoC in the Kashmir sector, this is not the case in Jammu. In the Jammu sector, people live in homes behind the fence and go across to their farms located ahead of the fence only for farming activities. They cultivate their land while armed soldiers stand guard.

Over the years, the presence of the Indian and Pakistani troops has increased on the LoC. Prior to such massive troop presence, locals also used to engage in raiding across the LoC. UNMOGIP used to report and deal with many such instances of petty robbery, smuggling of contraband, cattle thieving and encroachments to cut grass from fields across the LoC in the 1950s and 1960s. Both India and Pakistan actively sought UNMOGIP's help in resolving such cases. But not any more. The fence has changed everything.

'Do you ever get caught in the crossfire between the armies on either side?' I asked the village headman of Behroti, looking intently at the army posts on either side. Bullets from both sides could easily reach them and wreak havoc. The elderly man caught hold of my hand and took me to a shrine under a tree and told me confidently, 'Do you see this pir baba's shrine? *Baba ki meher hai* [Thanks to the blessings of the baba], we never get shot at.' He added that during the 1965 India–Pakistan war, guns which fired at the village were jammed and hence soldiers on either side tend to avoid firing at the civilian population here.

Clearly, I was unconvinced. So I kept asking for facts. It turned out that he was right. No one had ever been shot by the Pakistani army in that village—only some cattle. People would generally be indoors during CFVs but being indoors hardly prevents one from being hit when high-calibre shells are being fired back and forth. This was puzzling to me but I didn't challenge the local belief that the pir baba had ensured that no shells fell on them. Faith is useful (even though I don't have it) and if faith helps duck shells, why challenge that belief? The pir baba, after all, had an instrumental value.

So I asked Gahlawat while we were returning to the army mess on a dirt road along the LoC: 'What's all this pir baba business in Behroti?'

'There is a simple explanation for this,' he said. 'The village is so close to the Pakistani side that there is no way that the Pakistani shells will be aimed at Behroti; doing so could have implications for the Pakistani village as well. So the 120-mm shells that the Pakistani side uses almost always overshoot the village and fall somewhere closer to the fence, which is behind the village. More so, CFVs are mostly carried out with long-range guns here rather than personal weapons.'

It was getting dark and the view of the lit-up LoC fence was mesmerizing. In December 2015, American space agency NASA released the 'Top 15 Space Station Earth Images of 2015'[3] as selected by its Johnson Space Center's Earth Observations team. One of the breathtaking images was of the beautifully lit LoC. The LoC looks lovely from the sky, but it means death and destruction on the ground. For the people of Behroti, the fence also solidifies a pre-existing identity crisis. For many of us, the fence provides a sense of security, but not for the people of Behroti. For them, only the pir baba provides security.

'I don't go around dispelling their belief in the pir baba,' said Gahlawat. 'I don't even explain the range and ballistic trajectories of 120-mm guns. In times such as this one needs a lot of faith merely for survival.'

Between Life and Death

Located hardly a kilometre away from each other, the two Indian Border Outposts (BOPs) near Border Pillar (BP) No. 1 in the Indian Punjab, both manned by the BSF, are evidently dissimilar in appearance. Around 500 metres to my right was a well-fortified post, guarded by BSF soldiers wearing bulletproof gear, their machine guns loaded and pointing at the Pakistani post. This was in contrast to the post on the left side of the pillar, where I was standing. BSF soldiers on the left looked more relaxed and didn't wear any bulletproof gear; they still had their guns pointed at the Pakistani post though. More so, the post on the left was a regular one, not fortified with reinforced material. Both the Indian BOPs face Pakistani posts across the border. BP No. 1 is the first pillar at the border between Jammu and Punjab where the IB between India and Pakistan begins, according to Pakistan. The Indian interpretation is different: it considers the border in Jammu to be the IB as well. While this terminology might sound inconsequential, it is this phraseological jugglery that causes firing here. The Indian post next to BP No. 1 in the Punjab sector is Dhinda Forward and the Pakistani post on the other side is called Chak Qazian.

Having been on a tour of the border areas with the BSF for the past several days, I was taken aback by the visible contrast between the posts on either side of BP No. 1. Border posts tend to have similar appearances, especially in the nearby locations. In J&K, for instance, posts and bunkers are typically well-fortified to withstand bullets and even shells. However, in places like Rajasthan or Gujarat, where no shots are ever fired across the line, posts are often made of ordinary material that would hardly withstand shells fired by the adversary.

I was travelling from Jammu to Punjab after spending a few days with the BSF formations on the Jammu border. I was now about to cross over to Punjab, where the BSF officials of the 97th battalion, based in Jammu, would 'hand me over' to the officers of the Punjab BSF. I had arrived at the Paharpur post a few hours ago for some much-needed lunch and rest. Around 3 p.m., officers from the BSF's Gurdaspur sector took me in their vehicle and crossed over to Punjab. On our way to Gurdaspur we decided to stop at a viewing spot between the two posts, and that's where I was struck by the unmissable contrast they presented.

When asked about the reason behind this, the BSF officer who was accompanying me said something very interesting:

'The post on your right (Paharpur Forward) falls in Jammu in J&K. Since the status of the border between India and Pakistan in J&K is disputed by Pakistan, there is a possibility of firing between the posts when ceasefire is violated by either side. However, the post on your left (Dhinda Forward) falls in Punjab where the boundary between India and Pakistan is not disputed by Pakistan and so there is no danger of fire breaking out between the two sides.'

He sounded indifferent to a scenario I found so shockingly bizarre. The distance between the two posts there is around 1 kilometre, and that is often the difference between life and death.

It was a period of lull and there had been no CFVs for the past couple of days. And yet there was palpable tension and insecurity all around, mixed with bravado and heightened doses of nationalism. There was a sense of suspense, fear and thrill among the young twenty-something soldiers posted there, an air of uncertainty about what might happen next. A quick burst of machine-gun fire might ring out any time, and they must take cover and fire back.

The soldiers at Dhinda Forward were from the BSF's Gurdaspur sector in Punjab, and the men at Paharpur Forward were from the Jammu BSF. The former is a peace posting and the latter is a hazardous one. Men posted in Chak Qazian, the Pakistani post on the other side, were from the Pakistan Rangers (Punjab), and had orders to fire at one of the Indian posts: the one on my right, Paharpur Forward; they would only be shot at by men at the Paharpur post. This was a carefully orchestrated symphony of death and destruction.

I asked one of the officers to explain the firing dynamics in greater detail. The firing is almost always between the BSF post in Jammu and the Pakistan Rangers' post. But occasionally a stray bullet finds its way to the Indian post in Punjab or in its vicinity. Unless the soldiers posted in Dhinda Forward, the Punjab post, think it is deliberate, they hold fire and don't respond. They merely take cover so as not to get hit by stray bullets. 'But it's invariably hard for these boys to see their comrades get hit in the Paharpur Forward post by Pakistani bullets and not to do anything about it,' the officer said. On the Pakistan side, the Rangers are careful not to target the post in Punjab while they are firing at the post in Jammu, so as to avoid the combined firepower of the two neighbouring Indian posts.

'Do you want to take a look at the enemy post? If you are lucky you might be able to spot some of them.' The officer's words suddenly reminded me of the time I travelled through the Ranthambore National Park in Rajasthan several years ago, trying to spot tigers. He handed me a pair of binoculars and I tried to spot an enemy, but in vain. The viewing point near BP No. 1 that I was at had markers which charted in metres how close or far the Pakistani posts were; these markers would aid the soldiers in deciding upon the kind of weapons they must use to get a target on the other side. I assumed the other side had the same.

The Sceptic Who Became a Friend

'Take a cab; don't go in the army vehicle. It's safer that way.' Colonel Gahlawat's advice sounded counter-intuitive at the time.

I resisted: 'Doesn't an army jeep make my trip more secure?'

'Trust me,' he said. I did, and took a cab to reach Kupwara from Bhimber Gali that morning.

The colonel and I had started off on the wrong foot, but went on to become good friends in a few days. Commissioned into the Indian Army in 2002, Gahlawat was the logistics guy for the Bhimber Gali brigade. This being his third tenure in J&K, he knew the area and its operational challenges well—it was not the best of places to be in, specially since he had a young family, but he nonetheless intended to make life better for the people who lived ahead of the fence, where the civil administration did not dare to step in. For the 'nowhere' people living near the LoC, who suffered an intense identity crisis, the colonel came to symbolize the Indian state.

Gahlawat wasn't too happy to see a JNU professor when I was led into his room at the Bhimber Gali brigade HQ. I was hit by a volley of irritable questions: 'JNU? What is Kanhaiya Kumar still doing there in his late twenties? And what does he have against the Indian Army? And what about all these anti-India slogans there?' It was June 2016, less than five months after the 'JNU incident', and the doctored clips played by unscrupulous media channels were still fresh in people's minds. The unfriendly colonel's hostile attitude irritated me as well. In retrospect, however, I would not blame him. From Kashmir to Bhuj in Gujarat, whichever army or BSF location I visited on the LoC or the IB, I was asked the exact same question. I would spend the first thirty minutes explaining what really happened in JNU on that fateful evening in January 2016, why men and women in their late twenties are still studying in JNU at the 'taxpayer's expense', etc., etc. There was no getting away from that. I would tell them that I had finished my own PhD in my late twenties and that's the kind of time it takes to get a PhD degree, and that when you teach history, political science, philosophy and logic, you can't expect students not to question the injustices and politics around them. For some reason, I came upon the fiercest critics of JNU in Gujarat, the home state of Prime Minister Modi. I don't think the correlation is anything more than spurious.

A spirited thirty-minute monologue delivered by me would not do much to convince them perhaps, but it would silence them momentarily: 'Let the law take its own course; let's discuss the objective of your visit here.' The important lesson that I have learnt from my tryst with the men in uniform is that while some of them are persuaded by the relentless media campaign to malign JNU, almost all of them are amenable to reason and logic. They would, for instance, agree with me when I would ask them rhetorically: 'If the Delhi police claim that JNU students raised anti-India slogans, why are they reluctant to file a charge sheet in the court?'

So Gahlawat wasn't the only one who was upset about JNU, and I would more readily engage with a man serving on the front lines of the LoC, braving bullets every day, than with a Mumbai- or Delhi-based media house spreading poison to satisfy their hunger for TRPs. The former fought to keep the nation safe, the latter sold nationalism to millions of unsuspecting citizens. There was another reason why I was gladly indulging him: Gahlawat was making a difference to the lives of people in Behroti and other surrounding villages. From liaising with the civil authorities to provide succour to the villagers and getting new roads constructed to ensuring that their kids go to school and encouraging the local youth to dream beyond the confines of their isolated hamlet, Gahlawat had taken it upon himself to do more than merely fulfil the traditional duties of an army officer. I had previously taken the view in my writings that it wasn't the army's job to perform civilian duties and that they should stay away from such activities. But in several places along the LoC, there would be no development activity if it were not for people like Gahlawat.

'Are you not afraid of being fired at by the Pakistani soldiers who must be watching you from the other side?' I asked him when he accompanied me to Behroti and the surrounding villages in his uniform in full view of the enemy side. He had a few weapon-bearing soldiers in tow but that wouldn't have protected him if the Pakistanis were to open fire. There had been no violations in the past few days but again that didn't mean there would be no firing on that particular day.

'Sometimes you've got to take chances. I hope you don't mind.' He looked at me as if to seek my permission for potentially getting shot by the Pakistani soldiers.

'Sure, of course,' I said, determined to hide my nervousness. When I met him in Delhi after a couple of years, I asked him again: 'Were you serious that day about taking chances?'

'I was,' he said.

'You say no infiltration happens here due to the absence of local support. Why do you guys fire at each other then?' I asked him while we were chatting over a cup of hot tea in his home in Bhimber Gali. Despite his tirade against JNU, he seemed to have taken a liking to me, and so he wanted his wife and young son to meet me. 'It's a cyclical affair,' he said. 'They fire, we fire, and the cycle goes on . . . Sometimes we don't even know why it happens . . . It just happens.' His rather straightforward statement worried me deeply for it revealed how irresponsible the two nuclear powers were in managing their contentious borders.

Establishments in New Delhi and Islamabad and the hyper-nationalist media on both sides have very skewed notions about CFVs. Even a cursory discussion with the men posted along the LoC would tell us a completely different story, stories which can rudely dispel our entrenched belief systems.

I took Gahlawat's advice and got myself a local taxi to take me to Kupwara, and travelled through those tricky terrains without any armed escort. On our way, I passed through some of the most breathtakingly beautiful places in Kashmir, including the snow-clad Pir Panjal mountain range. There was fresh snowfall, mesmerizing waterfalls, deep blue valleys and colourful, barren, rocky mountains.

While passing through Kashmir's mofussil towns like Pampore and Shopian, we came across unsmiling young men sitting around looking closely at all the vehicles that passed by. Not long after I returned to New Delhi, terrorists belonging to the Lashkar-e-Taiba ambushed a Central Reserve Police Force (CRPF) convoy at Frestbal near Pampore in Srinagar on the Srinagar–Jammu National Highway. Eight CRPF personnel were killed and around twenty were injured in the attack. The media reported that 'The militants fired indiscriminately at the CRPF bus and also deflated its tyres.'

I called up Gahlawat to thank him for his life-saving advice.

One of Their Own

Academics who work on national security are a singularly disadvantaged lot—what they need is often classified; those in charge of that information guard it fiercely; if they ask around too much, they might be subjected to the occasional unwanted company; and if they happen to have information that they are not supposed to have, then they are automatically in violation of the archaic Official Secrets Act, a ridiculous British-era law. Over the years, I have found two ways of circumventing such disadvantages: first, by extensively interacting with retired officials from multiple organizations, and from both sides of the border. Second, by going on extensive field trips. What is surprising is how willing the people on the ground are to host you and to tell or show you things you have never seen or heard of.

In that sense then, travelling with the Indian Army and the BSF along the LoC in J&K, and the IB in Punjab, Rajasthan and Gujarat, was both a learning and humanizing experience—it humanized the border, the people who inhabit those inhospitable terrains, their stories and tribulations; it also humanized the men (and the occasional women) in uniform, their stories, their struggles, hopes and aspirations. One comes across life-changing experiences during such journeys, impressions one carries back home to bottle up in those large, colourful glass jars of memory—which one opens once in a while for a quick look so as to not lose touch with reality and human travails.

Among several such memories, one stands out and brings tears to my eyes whenever I think of it. During a field visit to the Bhuj area in June 2016, Tanvi Kulkarni, my colleague and PhD student, and I were told by BSF officials about the capture of a group of Pakistani fishermen on 11 May 2016. They were apprehended by the BSF along with two wooden fishing boats in a creek area. That sounded routine, except when we looked at the paperwork which our BSF liaison officer showed us after some persuasion. What we found shocked us.

Of the eighteen members of the group who hailed from the Thatta district of Pakistan in Sindh, six were minors: Abas, who had come along with his father Anwar was merely five years old; and Yassim, who had accompanied his father in the wooden boat, was eight years old. 'Five years old?' I asked the officer, shaken since my son was five at the time. 'What did Abas say when you arrested him?'

'Will I get some food?' was apparently what young Abas had asked the BSF men who apprehended the boat that had strayed into Indian waters. They might not have eaten for some time, hence the question, I reasoned.

'But how can a five-year-old survive a jail?' I asked, persisting with my questions. The officer assured us that Abas and the other young detainees would be put up with their fathers or relatives who had accompanied them on the treacherous journey through the creeks of Bhuj.

'They know when they enter the Indian waters, so it's not inadvertent crossing,' he said.

Why would they then take such a risk, of potentially having their young children arrested and thrown into jail? I was puzzled.

'Extreme poverty,' the officer answered. 'Even their mothers know of the risks involved, but they think young kids should go with their fathers and learn the trade rather than facing poverty at home.'

When asked about their whereabouts and what might happen to them, BSF officials said that they were handed over to the local police and were being held at the Joint Interrogation Centre (JIC) in Bhuj, where they would be quizzed by various intelligence agencies. Once the agencies were satisfied that they were harmless fishermen, they would be sent to Jaipur for counselling by the Pakistan High Commission and would eventually be sent back through the Wagah–Attari border. The whole process could take up to three to six months, even for a five-year-old. The officer wasn't visibly upset about it but he was curious about my feelings.

Tanvi and I spent the rest of the afternoon persuading the officer to let us meet Abas. 'Why?' asked the officer, curious. He had seen so many such cases that it had all become routine.

'I have a son about the same age,' I responded. But I told him I also wanted to write about it. He came up with a creative solution. He would have access to the boy, given his job. He promised to take us inside the detention centre, provided we could convince the Gujarat police guards at the gate that we were his junior officers accompanying him to observe and learn interrogation techniques. He would tell the guards as much, but we would have to act accordingly for the entry—'Provided,' he said, 'you don't write about it. If you take this route, you will never write about it . . . If you want to write about it, you can't come with me.' To visit or not to visit Abas was a major moral dilemma for me. The choice was simple: I could either have a fascinating story to tell or I could see him.

The story that I would write would mean almost nothing to him, or to anyone for that matter—it would only mean something to me, provide me with the self-serving joy of storytelling. As a writer, the allure of that perfect story can sometimes complicate what should be an easy decision to make. My dilemma was not unlike that of a war photographer engaged in precision photography—when soldiers are getting killed in action all around you, do you put down your camera and try to help or do you ignore your feelings and do your job, which is to simply capture the image and transmit it? The images you capture belong to your employer; and the moral angst is yours to keep.

I made the regrettable decision of not visiting Abas. When I look back at that moment today, I think I should have simply grabbed the opportunity, if only to reassure the boy that he would be sent home soon. Or to give him some chocolates, just to witness the joy on his face; how my own son would have jumped up in happiness at the sight of chocolates. That would have been some memory, besides being the source of a little vicarious pleasure.

'What do you think I should do?'

Tanvi seemed ambivalent about it. 'Your call,' she said, leaving the moral dilemma squarely to me, perhaps realizing how emotionally invested I was in the little boy's fate—or maybe she wanted no part in it. It was not that she wasn't affected by the absurdity of Abas's predicament. I knew she was, but the moral dilemma seemed entirely mine.

The Pakistan Connection

Nationalizing Hate

States fight. Warfare is partly their very raison d'être. In fact, a close reading of modern European history tells us that states were born out of relentless wars. War-making led to the creation of modern Western states. The celebrated American historian Charles Tilly historicizes and thereby demystifies modern states whose existence we often take for granted and whose fusion with nationalism has become one of the insurmountable challenges of our age. Where states once engaged in war fighting and the rhetoric of war mostly to survive, today statesmen mostly engage in them for domestic political reasons and to satisfy 'popular will'. War is often a sport and offers a national catharsis. Tilly's bare-bones account of modern state formation—that wars made states—both fascinated and worried me when I first read it during my university days, as a young student.

Interestingly, the very same states that violently fight each other, and shed the blood of their young, are also able to sit around a table to negotiate peace deals, often with humour and fun. Drinks, statesmanship and sophisticated cultural performances often accompany such stately occasions. That's because seasoned statesmen/stateswomen understand that war-making and deal-making are an essential part of modern statecraft—two sides of the same coin. There is a time to fight, and then there's a time to make peace. There are no permanent enemies of permanent friends—only interests are permanent.

So far so good. The trouble begins when they co-opt citizens in their war-making efforts, by sensationalizing war, by whipping them up into a frenzy against the opponent and by getting them to hate the 'Other', thereby nationalizing wars. States do so, to extrapolate Tilly's theory, to 'extract more resources' for war-making efforts. When ordinary citizens are co-opted into the war-making efforts of states in the age of instant communication and social media, war becomes a thriving hate industry. The soul of societies gets corrupted by the soot of hate. Because people might not understand the intricacies and nuances of statecraft, they often view the 'enemy' state vis-à-vis themselves in binaries, without considering the grey areas. Wars are fought on the basis of 'us vs them' arguments even as statesmen understand that in the real world the 'us vs them' logic doesn't hold.

Once they are part of the state-run hate industry, citizens assimilate hate and make it part of their identity and are unable to extricate themselves from it, even when states and statesmen move on, with their 'interests' taken care of or in pursuit of new ones.

Something very similar may have happened in the case of India and Pakistan. India and Pakistan have fought wars, negotiated treaties and used each other for domestic political purposes. When they fight each other, they do so wholeheartedly—well, almost (remember those Indo-Pak backchannel parleys while the Kargil conflict was raging on?). During times of relative peace and dialogue processes, they behave as if they never fought with each other.

When they are not at each other's throats, the Indian and Pakistani elites— the political and bureaucratic classes—share jokes, alcohol and a keen love for shayari, as civilized people anywhere should. But the general population and the media houses not fully schooled in the nuances of statecraft seem unable to make such dramatic shifts in perception, from enmity to friendship, from war to peace: the general population, thanks to caged nationalist narratives, and the media because they cater to and thrive on the charged-up emotions of the masses. The barriers that get built during times of tension are almost never demolished, making the general population in India and Pakistan prisoners of their prejudices; it's unfortunate that they hardly get a chance to meet each other and thus bust the myths they believe about each other.

Then comes a time when the states propose to make peace, once again, and sensibly so. This time the caged populations with their hardened prejudices and hate react with anger and cynicism. 'How can we talk to them?' they ask. 'They have killed our countrymen.' This is when the half-truths and self-serving platitudes that the states and their elites have been peddling come to bite them in the back. They become victims of their own propaganda. National hate campaigns come a full circle and states and their elites find themselves in a political fix. Recall the domestic political and popular reactions when Prime Minister Modi tried to reach out to Pakistan by going on an unannounced visit to Lahore in December 2015. Now contrast this with the support he received for the 2016 surgical strikes against Pakistan. 'Enmity isn't helpful. They are people like us; let's talk and resolve our problems,' the political class might reason, with maturity and statesmanship. But that makes no difference now: 'You are an anti-national,' the enraged citizens respond.

This is perhaps what happened between India and Pakistan, wherein both sides seem to have nationalized hate.

We have reached the 'you are an anti-national' stage, with the public demanding retribution and bloodshed, and considering anyone even advocating talks with Pakistan to be working against the interests of the nation. Consider the comments on social media or the commentary in the 'letters to the editor' section of national dailies. Statesmen either play to the gallery, promising to offer bloodshed ('We should get ten Pakistani heads') or scurry for cover if they think they can't keep up with the frenzy of the times. Those even attempting to reason with the enraged masses will be called names. When the issue of Indian soldier Lance Naik Hemraj's beheading allegedly by the Pakistan Army was raging on, a senior Indian cabinet minister told me that 'both sides engage in such activities and my people have told me so'.

'So why don't you make a statement and calm things down?' I asked him.

'I can't mention this in public. It would have grave implications for me,' was his response. Such is the fury of nationalist forces.

The Enemy Trap

It was in mid-2004, around fourteen years ago, that I first participated in an Indo-Pak track-II dialogue in Kathmandu, the capital of Nepal. As a young student and uninitiated rookie, I was naturally at the bottom of the food chain, a note taker, magnanimously called a rapporteur, in that Pugwash conference on J&K. The conference, which was organized with the blessings of both the Indian and Pakistani governments, had brought together Kashmiris from both sides as well as participants from mainland India and Pakistan. I took down the notes of the proceedings with great alacrity and sincerity—perhaps a bit too much of both. A retired

Indian ambassador with unforgivingly hawkish views about Pakistan was deeply upset about how I had jotted down the views of the participants without sugar-coating what was said: 'The rapporteur's report reads as if it is written by ISPR,' he said, referring to the Pakistan Army's public relations wing. 'How could this silly university student torpedo the Indian position on Kashmir!' he must have thought.

'I merely reported what went on in the meeting ensuring that I missed out nothing,' I feebly murmured in my defence. His one statement had a damning effect on what I had spent the entire previous night working on, literally burning the midnight oil. I was both disappointed and embarrassed, almost wanting to run for cover—it was my first time being called 'a Pakistani', which is akin to being called a traitor. It looked as if my track-II career was practically over with that one meeting.

During the evening cocktails, another retired Indian diplomat—thoughtful, wise and tactful—patted my shoulder while I was still trying to recover my 'Indian identity' by sticking to the Indian participants, judiciously avoiding the Pakistanis and staying away from the Kashmiri dissidents. 'Writing a rapporteur's report can often be a painful experience,' said Mohammad Hamid Ansari, who later became the vice president of India. He took me to a corner of the ballroom at the Hyatt Regency hotel and told me, 'What needs to be kept in mind, however, is that the report needs to reflect the spirit of the discussion rather than a verbatim account of the discussions. Verbatim accounts are almost always explosive, especially in conflict situations such as this.' Ansari's wise words have stood me in good stead ever since. The sour note that my track-II journey started on was not entirely unexpected; most track-II efforts continue to have a bad reputation in India.

Not just peace-building with Pakistan via track-II dialogues, almost everything Pakistani has a bad reputation in India, including academic research on Pakistan unless, of course, you take the official 'line'.

Researching contemporary Pakistan is one of the toughest intellectual endeavours in contemporary India. For one, there is very little expertise on Pakistan in the country, notwithstanding the daily 'Pakistan debates' that take place inside the Indian TV studios. Systematic intellectual inquiry requires reasoned and dispassionate analysis and, equally importantly, access to archives and interviewees in Pakistan. Indian academics often hesitate to put forth an objective stand on the subject of Pakistan and Indo-Pak relations. The tendency, an easy escape route as it is, is to toe the *sarkari* (government) line on Pakistan, i.e., to define Pakistan as an army-ruled, soon-to-fail, quasi-theocratic state which is out to destroy India. If you abide by this straightforward assumption in some shape or form, your analysis would be broadly acceptable. If you challenge it, you might not find much acceptability either with officialdom or among the public. Indian officials might not entertain you, retired ones will tell you that you have too little policy experience, fellow academics will sneer at your 'lack of data and material' and the general public will look at you with disbelief—'How can you say such [neutral] things about Pakistan!'

As a result, most Indian academics and researchers tend to study Pakistan from within the nationalist echo chambers of New Delhi, and don't even make efforts to go to Pakistan. The story is hardly different in the case of Pakistani academics. Going to Pakistan does come attached with a certain stigma. Then comes the challenge of access—accessing Pakistan, its people, experts and archives. The army, the ISI and its officialdom in general are equally suspicious of India and

Indians, even though Pakistanis in general are increasingly far more welcoming of Indians than vice versa.

This shouldn't be surprising given how the Indian understanding of Pakistan is fed a steady diet of anti-Pakistan hate by the country's mainstream media houses. While this has broadly been the case since at least the beginning of the Kashmir insurgency, India's popular imaginings of Pakistan have been on steroids since the country's victory at Kargil. Kargil fundamentally transformed India's view of Pakistan in several ways. Kargil coalesced the multitude of Indian narratives about Pakistan into one cohesive story: the back-stabbing by the Pakistanis, how India taught Pakistan a lesson, how the valorous victory at Kargil was arrived at, etc. Even Bollywood's portrayal of Indian nationalism and the Pakistani 'Other' can be categorized into pre-Kargil and post-Kargil eras.

What this then means is that if one wants to research Pakistan or Indo-Pak relations, especially from a security angle, one's got to be tenacious, adventurous and willing to brazen it out.

Those Indians and Pakistanis who know each other and their countries well and have fond memories of each other are quickly fading away into oblivion. They are no longer prominent in their respective countries' national discourses, and are hardly a part of the vanguard negotiating bilateral relations between the two sides—they seem clueless about how to grapple with the absurd portrayals of the other side. They seem to have given up in exasperation.

In short, here in India we inhabit a decidedly warped intellectual space—created by our fears, inadequacies and, sometimes, pettiness—that severely restricts our understanding of the 'Other'. Pakistan and India will continue to be each other's bête noire for a very long time, even after the two states and their deep states realize the futility of being so. Partition may have separated Pakistan from India, but the two countries do not seem to be in the mood to let go of each other. The more we hate each other, the more the 'Other' plays a role in our national lives.

Pakistan's deep state, thanks to its self-defeating obsession with Kashmir, has landed India in an enemy trap, one from which we are unable to extricate ourselves. It has not only prevented us from thinking freely and objectively about one of the deadliest and oldest conflicts in the world, but has also brought the worst in us out in the open. Pakistan holds a mirror to the dark underbelly of our societal self as we find ourselves in an enemy trap. India's Pakistan fixation is slowly and steadily transforming us—not in a good way.

Journeys to Pakistan

'Beware of the Pakistan Army—they will turn you,' one retired Indian Army general told me with a mischievous smile on his moustached face, just as I was about to set out to see the Pakistani side of the LoC. 'They even managed to turn our people inside the Indian embassy in Islamabad . . . it's easier on the outside. And you are civilian with no counter-intelligence exposure.' He was referring to former Indian High Commission official Madhuri Gupta who was arrested, and later convicted, for passing on Indian state secrets to Pakistani intelligence agencies in 2010.[1] Almost everyone who knew of my visit to the LoC with the Pakistan Army cautioned me that I should be careful as there were inherent dangers in doing what I was going to do. With almost everyone who cautioned me against travelling with the Pakistan Army, I flagged a complicated notion of national interest to justify my visit: 'Knowing the views of the Pakistan Army, seeing their side of the LoC, visiting their border villages and hearing about the current state of Indo-Pak relations from the horse's mouth in GHQ would indirectly serve our national interest,' I argued. I was hinting at the idea that the pursuit of national interest is a complex affair. In one sense, that's the beauty of national interest—the contents of it are not static, only the idea of it is.

In a certain sense, I told them, there is a pertinent need to know the 'enemy', without the knowledge of whom there is no way a proper national strategy can be formulated, and academics such as myself could potentially add to that endeavour by excavating facts, examining them and offering analysis dispassionately. The two countries can't go on behaving like children who refuse to talk to each other after a fight; as former NSA Shivshankar Menon put it: 'Katti isn't policy.' [2]

Travelling to Pakistan is like going on an intellectual pilgrimage. You need to prepare for it, mentally and psychologically, and hope that everything goes fine, both in Pakistan and back in India, and between them. You need to emotionally invest in it. Everyone would have something to say about the 'spiritual' experience that's awaiting you there. You need to have the fortitude and wisdom to discern what is important and what is not and the limits of intellectual pursuits. And yet, no matter how many bases you try to cover, the pilgrimage ends up taking its own course —it's a personal journey and nothing can prepare you for it. Just as they say about war, 'No plan survives the first shot.' The best preparation then is to be intellectually curious, open-minded and to know one's moral and intellectual limits, and of course, to make extensive field notes and take photos of those notes every evening using your phone, and email them to yourself.

I have been to Pakistan around ten times, mostly for conferences and meetings and a couple of times for fieldwork.

It's been a thrilling experience every time, as thrilling as my first visit to the north of India from a small hill town in Kerala at the age of sixteen. At that age, in the northern Indian city of Meerut I encountered another India where everything was so totally different—the language, the cuisine, the way people dressed and how they lived. I was thrilled despite the chaos and the confusion, and the contrast with the part of the south I had come from. My feelings on Pakistan aren't much different, and I continue to be just as thrilled.

The most memorable of my journeys to Pakistan, excluding the one to the LoC, was the one I took in March 2006. A Pugwash delegation from India had requested a meeting with General Pervez Musharraf. He was the President of the country and its army chief, making him an exceptionally formidable Pakistani leader whose power those days was hardly challenged, and popular sentiment favoured him. Musharraf was then in the prime of his career and we were told by Lieutenant General Talat Masood, a member of the Pugwash Council and an adviser to Musharraf, that the meeting was organized in the Aiwan-e-Sadr, the seat of Pakistan's presidency, located in Islamabad between the Parliament building and the Cabinet block of the Pakistan Secretariat. We send our request through Talat, and within a few hours came the invite to meet Musharraf.

And just like that, one morning we were driven up the Constitution Avenue in the heart of Islamabad to meet the President, who was born in Delhi before moving to Pakistan as a child with his family. Around forty of us, including the Pakistani delegates, were seated in a large hall, shortly after which Musharraf turned up with Talat by his side. He wore his army uniform, and looked warm, hospitable and charming. He walked up to each delegate, shook hands and, looking into his/her eyes, said, 'Hello. Pervez. Welcome to Pakistan', waited for a response and posed for photographs. He flagged his favourite Kashmir formula once again and reiterated that he would be happy to talk to Indian stakeholders anywhere and any time. 'I am committed to resolving the Kashmir dispute and making peace between India and Pakistan. Imagine what can happen between our countries if we convert into a zone of peace, free trade and people-to-people interaction. It can herald cooperation and peace not just between us, but the entire region will be transformed.' Musharraf was at his persuasive best and he was keen on selling his Kashmir formula—in fact, it wasn't a mere sales pitch. In the past, he had reached out to both New Delhi and Kashmir. He'd met the Kashmiri dissident leadership in various world capitals, including Dubai, to discuss his solution with them. Most of them were delighted to be consulted, and were happily on board—except Syed Ali Shah Geelani, the hard-line Hurriyat leader. It's ironical because Geelani is the most pro-Pakistan of them all and yet he disagreed with Musharraf. He thought Musharraf was selling out Pakistan's Kashmir cause.

Once Musharraf was out of power, his Kashmir solution found no takers in Pakistan including in the Pakistan Army. While the Pakistan People's Party (PPP) which succeeded him claimed that there was no paper trail of the discussions, several members of the Pakistan Army went on to state that in various track-II forums where I was present Musharraf was negotiating on his own accord, that he had not taken the Pakistan Army top brass on board in the Kashmir solution.

At the fag end of the two-hour luncheon meeting, one of us got up and said, 'Mr President, we are delighted to be in Pakistan. We would like to visit Azad Kashmir . . . Could you please allow us to visit at least Mirpur?'

'Why not? Do visit. We are doing great work there, you will see it yourself,' he responded enthusiastically. He seemed pleased with the reference to 'Azad Kashmir' by an Indian delegate, which one wouldn't normally hear given that India officially refers to it as 'PoK'.

'We don't have visas to go there, Mr President,' the delegate persisted.

'Not to worry, I will make arrangements for you.' He turned to one of his aides and murmured something into the man's ears. The visit was arranged in a few hours.

We set out to 'Azad Kashmir' the following morning, without a visa. We could see several cars piloting and tailing us through the journey. At one point, the same delegate who got us permission from Musharraf stepped out of the bus and asked the men in one of the cars why they were following us. Not that he didn't know who they were.

'We are merely ensuring your safety,' the men told him. They never once left our company till we got back to the Serena Hotel in Islamabad. They sat through the meetings that we had with the local journalists in Mirpur, meals that we had at the homes of local friends and during our public meeting that was organized by Justice Abdul Majeed Malik (retired), the former chief justice of the Azad Jammu Kashmir Supreme Court. We, especially the Kashmiris from the Indian side, received a warm welcome there. There was hope in the air that the two sides of the (erstwhile) princely state of J&K would unite soon, even if nominally. Those were indeed thrilling and hopeful times.

Another memorable incident took place in March 2008. I was part of an Indian delegation in Islamabad which included Mehbooba Mufti, who later went on to become J&K's chief minister; her deputy from the BJP, Nirmal Singh; Omar Abdullah, who also later became the chief minister; and Sajjad Lone, who became a minister in the Mufti cabinet, among others. On the morning of 28 March, Mehbooba Mufti asked me if I was willing to accompany her to Asif Ali Zardari's home in Islamabad. His wife and PPP leader, Benazir Bhutto, had just been assassinated three months ago. I was keen to meet him, so I went along with Mufti to the Zardari House in Islamabad. Zardari, who was soon to be the President of Pakistan, came out and warmly greeted us. After exchanging pleasantries, he asked Mufti who I was. She hadn't expected the question but gathered her wits and said, 'My political adviser.'

We had an hour-long meeting over tea and biscuits. The PPP had just won the elections on a huge sympathy wave. Given that his party was about to make government soon, Zardari said he was ready to talk about Kashmir, ready to think out of the box in order to resolve the issue and ready to 'do business' with India on Kashmir. He promised that his government would take steps to establish mutually beneficial commercial and economic projects in the erstwhile princely state of J&K in consultation with the Government of India.

Zardari treated us very well and gave us signed copies of Bhutto's book *Reconciliation: Islam, Democracy, and the West*.[3] When we emerged from his house, something very unexpected happened. Zardari, Mufti and the latter's 'political adviser' were surrounded by the local media, who had rushed to the Zardari House hearing that Mufti, the president of the Jammu and Kashmir People's Democratic Party (JKPDP) which was at the time a coalition partner in the J&K government, was visiting Zardari. I tried to get away from the cameras but one of Zardari's aides asked me to stand next to Mufti, which I did. Zardari introduced her as his sister from Kashmir. Both Mufti and Zardari told the surrounding journalists that the future of Kashmir should be seen in terms of it being a bridge of commerce and trade and other mutually beneficial interactions between the two countries. As usual, some Pakistani journalists were trying to provoke Mufti by raising the issue of human rights violations. Zardari cut them off and said that his sister was visiting him with a message of peace.

In 2006, our delegation had included Omar Abdullah, who during the visit had had a private meeting with General Musharraf, the President. One evening, the Indian delegation was hosted at the local press club in Islamabad. While we were coming out to return to the Serena Hotel, local scribes started heckling Omar Abdullah whose father, Farooq Abdullah, was the chief minister of J&K at the time. Some among the assembled journalists hurled abuse at him. 'You have killed and persecuted innocent Kashmiris. What kind of a Muslim are you?' they shouted. Abdullah froze and the Pakistani minister of foreign affairs Khurshid Mahmud Kasuri, who was with the Indian delegation at the time, tried pacifying the situation but without much success. It was high drama and confusion and the Indians seemed embarrassed, as did our Pakistani hosts. That's when JKPDP leader and a prominent Kashmiri Shia leader, Molvi Iftikhar Hussain Ansari, a well-educated Islamic theologian and firebrand speaker, spoke up. He raised his voice, rebuked the Pakistani journalists and challenged them on Islam. 'What do you know about Islam?' he asked. 'I will tell you what Islam is, come debate with me.' He blasted them for several minutes in his angry and loud voice, all the while imparting the lessons of Islam.

My journey to the LoC as a guest of the Pakistan Army was one week long. 'Can they do in seven days what the good Jesuits couldn't do in six years, that too with the help of God?' I'd responded to the general who cautioned me to 'beware of the Pakistan Army—they will turn you'. My six years in Catholic seminaries weren't enough to brainwash me.

That was another reason why I wasn't too worried about the ISI's chances of success at turning me.

The 'Why' Question

Once a serving Pakistani diplomat hosted me for dinner. At the end of a long conversation about the idea of India, the disturbing rise of the right wing, the state of minorities in the country, left politics in Kerala and the left-liberal citadel called JNU, the diplomat, to my utter shock, said, 'So you are a Christian from Kerala, educated at JNU—no wonder you write what you write!' I quickly spoke up and corrected the distinguished diplomat: 'Nope, I write what I write because of my political convictions. More so, I write critically on India's foreign policy because I firmly believe that doing so is in my country's enlightened national interest.' That one incident from a decade ago rushes back to me whenever someone tries to conflate my arguments with my identity. Sometimes, it also affects how I think others see me and how that shapes and affects me. Identities are like stubborn biases—howsoever much one tries to shed them, they persist, hovering just below the surface of our mindscape. The job of an academic is to recognize the chains of identity that tie one down, and minimize their pull on one's intellectual inquiry. You can't avoid them, but you may be able to moderate their influence if you recognize them.

Getting invited by two warring armies, especially when you are not from a third, 'neutral' country, is an uphill task. Both of them have apprehensions about the 'unknown' entity that you are. 'Malayali, Christian, left-leaning JNU professor' is indeed such an entity, or so they think. Both sides are a bit puzzled as to why the other side has agreed to host you. But then the 'unknownness' has its peculiar charm, an ability to arouse a certain curiosity in the mind of the onlooker.

The hosts know that academic scholarship has its own true utility, even though academics might not habitually take sides, as they shouldn't. Extending an invite, ultimately, comes down to weighing the doubt against the utility. The Indian Army did consider the odds and ponder over them, and eventually it took the efforts of a courageous and visionary army general, who essentially acted on his own, for me to get my invite. When I was with the Indian side, I never once felt out of place; I was one of them, among brothers.

For the Pakistani side too, I was an unknown entity. 'Malayali, Christian, left-leaning JNU professor' may be appealing to them, but with it comes the dilemma of the guest not toeing the party line. Getting someone like that into your midst is taking a risk, albeit a reasonable one. Why would they take that risk? Perhaps because, as a Pakistani friend put it, 'Given the bad press that Pakistan gets on a daily basis, even neutral writing by an Indian will be viewed as good news by the Pakistan Army.' So for them, it made sense.

One of the major reasons for all the organizations involved for inviting me, I suppose, was the desire to not be left behind. Once the Indian Army had invited me to the LoC, the BSF, whose story is hardly ever written about, didn't want to be left behind. Hence while the army hosted me for less than a week, the BSF offer was for close to three weeks. It was armed with these two sets of experiences that I approached the Pakistan Army to host me—'So that my work is not one-sided,' I argued.

The 'why' question is not only about the gaze of the other. It is also about one's own moral–political predicaments. About the pursuit of intellectual endeavours and their limits and attendant dilemmas. About constantly redefining one's own sense of national interest and its limits. About exploring whether one's nation's interest can coexist with that of the adversary's. About the contradictions inherent to such an inquiry and the attempts to resolve them, which most often end up being futile.

The Lives on the Line

Visiting both sides of the LoC manned by rival armies was definitely one hell of a personal experience for me—but it was also much more than that. While recounting it, as I have in the previous pages, one cannot overstate the underlying tragedy engulfing the borderlands and their inhabitants. My journey was about witnessing the lived experiences of thousands of people who tragically live within the flight path of artillery shells. During the high tide of Indo-Pak tensions, they count the days of their lives, one at a time. On relatively peaceful days, they stare at the homes of their relatives across the notional line guarded by armed soldiers, for all they can possibly do is stare. On a long-range time span, they become cognizant of what the LoC has done to their lives, personally and professionally, the lives they could have had had it not been for it.

Violent death and grave injuries aren't the only tragedies one witnesses in these treacherous borderlands: ordinary villagers get caught in the middle of competing nationalisms and bear the costs of national catharsis. They are the sacrificial lambs of our respective national pride and prejudices.

Travelling along the LoC, one realizes the arbitrariness of the factors that govern the lives of the people who reside there. Like the tributary of a river, the LoC twists and turns, a man-made current that is slowly sweeping away any sense of normalcy the people of these villages cling to. Generation after generation, they are at the receiving end of wars, hyper-nationalism and military manoeuvres. It's a violent normal for them. The older generations have seen normalcy in their younger years—they know there's something beyond what they witness now. But what about those young kids who have been born and brought up there? Those who haven't experienced normalcy and peace in their whole lives? How would it feel to be a kid who thinks that running for cover when bullets rain on them is what constitutes a great part of one's life? And that it is normal? What would that kid grow up into?

The men who serve along the LoC have the luxury of not having to live there for the rest of their lives, unlike the villagers. But they are also, in a sense, the victims of the failures of our political classes. Young men in their early twenties are sent to man the LoC, to kill, be killed and see villagers on either side get killed. For some, it's just a job; some others feel the pain but are helpless.

The LoC, then, marks the collective failure of the Indian and Pakistani nations. It's tragedy, hubris and hyper-nationalism all rolled into one, making it one of the most dangerous places on earth.

Acknowledgements

Having been trained as an academic, and told not to write in the first person, most of my writings tend to be academic and/or policy-oriented, stuff that most people do not read. I don't blame them—why would someone read a work if it's not fun reading it? When I returned from the Pakistani side of the LoC in December last year, I decided to write about my visit, and was determined to do so in a 'readable' manner.

I suggested to Penguin's Ranjana Sengupta that I was keen on writing a travelogue on my travels with the Indian and Pakistani armed forces along the LoC and the Indo-Pak IB. Ranjana agreed: So I must thank her for trusting an academic to pull off a 'readable' travelogue.

This book is a spin-off from a larger academic study I have been engaged in for the past several years which aimed to examine and explain ceasefire violations between India and Pakistan along the J&K border. I remain grateful to all those who helped me in my intellectual journey to understand why the LoC remains as dangerous as it is.

My travels to either side of the LoC/IB (and this book) would not have been possible without the sustained support of senior Indian and Pakistani military officers, both serving and retired. I thank the Border Security Force (BSF) officials who organized my field visits to Jammu, Punjab, Rajasthan, and Gujarat; Northern Command of the Indian Army, Lt. Gen. (retd) D.S. Hooda in particular, for helping me with field visits in Kashmir; and finally, the Pakistan Army for the field visits to the Pakistani side of the LoC, and to the General Headquarters, Rawalpindi. I thank Lt. Gen. (retd) Tariq Waseem Ghazi, Lt. Gen (retd) Aditya Singh, Lt. Gen. (retd) Waheed Arshad and Mr Aditya Mishra of the BSF for facilitating my visits to the Indian-Pakistan border areas.

I am thankful to Nicholas Rixon for his tips on how to write a travelogue, and Gaurav Saini, Tanvi Kulkarni and Manu Sharma for telling me how to make this book less boring to their generation.

I am grateful to member of Parliament Dr Shashi Tharoor, the former chief minister of J&K Omar Abdullah, Lt. Gen. (retd) Ata Hasnain of the Indian Army and Lt. Gen. (retd) Asad Durrani of the Pakistan Army for writing short, thoughtful endorsements for the book.

Finally, I thank all those serving officers and soldiers of the Indian and Pakistani armies and the BSF for hosting me in their mess halls, barracks and bunkers, and answering my often irritating and persistent questions.

Notes

Prologue

1. For data on CFVs and resultant casualties, see Indo-Pak Conflict Monitor, 'Ceasefire Violations', http://indopakconflictmonitor. org/cfv.php.
2. For more on the concept of mass media and manufacturing of consent, see Edward S. Herman and Noam Chomsky, *Manufacturing Consent: The Political Economy of the Mass Media* (New York: Pantheon Books, 1988).
3. For data on CFVs and resultant casualties, see Indo-Pak Conflict Monitor, 'Ceasefire Violations', http://indopakconflictmonitor. org/cfv.php.
4. 'WATCH: Indian Army Destroys Pakistani Bunkers at LoC', Zee News, published on 7 May 2017, https://www.youtube. com/watch?v=DCC7JGjzvEw

Chapter 1: Inside the Enemy Territory

1. 'PM Narendra Modi, Mani Shankar Aiyar, Gujarat Elections and Pakistan: Everything You Need to Know', *Indian Express*, 11 December 2017, https://indianexpress.com/elections/ gujarat-assembly-elections-2017/pm-narendra-modi-mani-shankar-aiyar-gujarat-elections-and-pakistan-everything-you-need-to-know/.
2. Ibid.
3. 'Manmohan Singh's Statement Full Text: "PM Modi Must Apologise to Nation to Restore Dignity of His Office"', *Indian*

Express, 11 December 2017, https://indianexpress.com/article/india/full-text-pm-modi-must-apologise-to-nation-to-restore-honour-of-his-office-says-manmohan-singh-4977980/.

4. 'Slammed by PM, Rapped by Rahul, Mani Shankar Aiyar Issues Lukewarm Apology', *Times of India*, 7 December 2017, https://timesofindia.indiatimes.com/india/slammed-by-pm-rapped-by-rahul-mani-shankar-aiyar-issues-lukewarm-apology/articleshow/61966234.cms.

5. 'Modi Can Never Become PM, Can Sell Tea: Mani Shankar Aiyar', *Indian Express*, 17 January 2014, https://indianexpress.com/article/india/politics/modi-can-never-become-pm-can-sell-tea-mani-shankar-aiyar/.

6. Rakesh Sinha, 'Manmohan Singh's Dinner with Pakistanis Is Unforgivable', *NDTV.com*, 12 December 2017, https://www.ndtv.com/opinion/manmohan-singhs-historic-mistake-in-dining-with-pakistanis-1786662.

7. 'Why Did PM Modi Go to Pakistan for Wedding in Sharif's Family, Asks Congress', *News18.com*, 10 December 2017, https://www.news18.com/news/politics/why-did-pm-modi-go-to-pakistan-for-wedding-in-sharifs-family-asks-congress-1600001.html.

Chapter 2: The Men Who Took Me to the Enemy Territory

1. Happymon Jacob and Kaveri Bedi, 'Patriot Games at Attari-Wagah', *The Hindu*, 21 August 2017, https://www.thehindu.com/opinion/lead/patriot-games-at-attari-wagah/article19530198.ece.

2. In July 1989, the two Prime Ministers had 'directed that the Defence Secretaries of India and Pakistan, should in their future meetings work towards a comprehensive settlement in accordance with the Simla agreement and that this settlement should be based on the redeployment of forces to reduce the chances of conflict and avoidance of the use of force, and further directed that the army authorities should continue discussions to determine future positions on the ground to which redeployment would take place so as to confirm to the Simla agreement and ensure durable peace in the area'. Joint Press Release, 17 July 1989.

3. Shyam Saran, *India Sees the World: Kautilya to the 21st Century* (New Delhi: Juggernaut Books, 2017).

4. The northernmost demarcated point of the LoC, under the Simla Agreement of 1972, is referred to as NJ9842. It falls in the Siachen sector.

Chapter 3: The Obstacle Course before the LoC

1. Shailaja Neelakantan, 'When NSA Ajit Doval Outlined India's New Pak Strategy—Defensive offense—Perfectly', *Times of India*, 4 October 2016, https://timesofindia.indiatimes.com/india/When-NSA-Ajit-Doval-outlined-Indias-new-Pakistan-strategy-defensive-offense-perfectly/articleshow/54670600.cms

Chapter 4: Guest of the Enemy Forces

1. Happymon Jacob, *Ceasefire Violations in Jammu and Kashmir: A Line on Fire*, (Washington, DC: United States Institute of Peace, 2017), https://www.usip.org/sites/default/files/PW131-Ceasefire-Violations-in-Jammu-and-Kashmir-A-Line-on-Fire.pdf. These causes of CFVs are further explained in my book *Line of Fire: Ceasefire Violations and India–Pakistan Escalation Dynamics* (New Delhi: Oxford University Press, forthcoming).
2. Albert Wohlstetter, 'The Delicate Balance of Terror', *Foreign Affairs* 37, no. 2 (1959): (pp. 211-234)
3. 'Army Commandos Cross LoC, Kill 3 Pak Soldiers', *Tribune*, 26 December 2017, https://www.tribuneindia.com/news/jammu-kashmir/army-commandos-cross-loc-kill-3-pak-soldiers/519170.html
4. For data on CFVs and resultant casualties, see Indo-Pak Conflict Monitor, 'Ceasefire Violations', http://indopakconflictmonitor.org/cfv.php.
5. Shujaat Bukhari, 'Deathtraps along the Border', *Friday Times*, 10 April 2015, http://www.thefridaytimes.com/tft/deathtraps-along-the-border/.
6. Peerzada Ashiq, 'More IED Blasts in India than in Afghanistan, Syria: Report', *Hindustan Times*, 7 May 2015, http://www.hindustantimes.com/india/more-ied-blasts-in-india-than-in-afghanistan-syria-report/story-a6OHsxDdjrmvvgL1R0YJvN.html (accessed on 10 June 2016).

7. Dennis Kux, *India and the United States: Estranged Democracies, 1941-1991*, p. 113 (New Delhi: Sage Publications, 1994).

8. http://www.un.org/Depts/DPKO/Missions/unmogip/ unmogipB.htm

9. Figures provided by the Travel and Trade Authority, Muzaffarabad, PoK, Pakistan.

Chapter 5: Inside the Rawalpindi Garrison

1. Discussion with Nirupama Subramanian via text message, January 2018.

Chapter 6: Among Brothers in Arms

1. Happymon Jacob, 'Disquiet on the Western front', *The Hindu*, 18 August 2016, https://www.thehindu.com/opinion/lead/ Disquiet-on-the-western-front/article14574579.ece.

2. 'Ceasefire Violations', *Press Information Bureau*, Ministry of Defence, Government of India, 11 December 2015, http://pib. nic.in/newsite/PrintRelease.aspx?relid=133036.

3. 'India-Pakistan Border at Night', digital image, in 'Top 15 Space Station Earth Images of 2015', *NASA.gov*, December 2015, https://www.nasa.gov/feature/top-15-earth-images-of-2015.

Chapter 7: The Pakistan Connection

1. 'Woman Diplomat Accused of Passing Secrets to Pakistan, Arrested', *Times of India*, 27 April 2010, https://timesofindia. indiatimes.com/india/Woman-diplomat-accused-of-passing-secrets-to-Pakistan-arrested/articleshow/5863761.cms

2. 'You Can't Tell Pakistan: Katti, We Won't Talk. Katti Isn't Policy, Says Ex-NSA Shivshankar Menon', *Indian Express*, 10 January 2016, https://indianexpress.com/article/india/india-news-india/ you-cant-tell-pak-katti-we-wont-talk-katti-isnt-policy-says-ex-nsa-shivshankar-menon/.

3. Benazir Bhutto, *Reconciliation: Islam, Democracy, and the West* (New York: Harper Perennial; reprint edition 2008).

Index

1. Travelogue, not a serious study of LoC
2. Recounts with an almost childlike undisguised pleasure how he did it.
3. Leveraged his contacts from Track II
4. At Muzaffarabad, We know all about you!
   (p 1)
5. Interesting snippets: no batmen,
6. Lengthy diversions into unrelated side stories such as how Aziz Ahmed Khan was appointed ambassador to India (p 9-10); China (p 32)
7. Irrelevant to general public but interesting to those who follow and know people in question
8. Interesting juxtaposition: Going on a field trip to Pak LoC — a JNU professor — at a time when a harmless dinner party had been made into a election punch (p 20)
9. "Call me if you need anything" Refrain.
10. The Vasant Vihar Man!
11. "The Men Who Took Me to Enemy Territory" VVM, Lt Gen Waheed Arshad (p 49)
    (Arshad revelation that Kargil Op "was Well Planned")
12. How minders in Pakistan told you — the aim being to let you know ur being watched. (p 65-66)
13. Like to call India Hindustan
14. "Tall lean man with sharp features! (p 79) The kind who kills without orders.
15. "It will be a pity if
16. (p 82) The dilemmas of HJS partisan. Anate
17. (p 93) Randomness of Life & Death on the LOC